Bob Becking
A Transverse Dreamer

Beihefte zur Zeitschrift für die alttestamentliche Wissenschaft

Edited by
John Barton, Reinhard G. Kratz, Nathan MacDonald,
Sara Milstein, and Markus Witte

Volume 552

Bob Becking

A Transverse Dreamer

—

Essays on the Book of Micah

DE GRUYTER

ISBN 978-3-11-120783-4
e-ISBN (PDF) 978-3-11-120865-7
e-ISBN (EPUB) 978-3-11-120931-9
ISSN 0934-2575

Library of Congress Control Number: 2023934068

Bibliographic information published by the Deutsche Nationalbibliothek
The Deutsche Nationalbibliothek lists this publication in the Deutsche Nationalbibliografie;
detailed bibliographic data are available on the internet at http://dnb.dnb.de.

Typsetting: Meta Systems Publishing & Printservices GmbH, Wustermark
Printing and binding: CPI books GmbH, Leck

www.degruyter.com

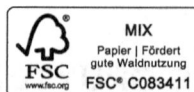

MIX
Papier | Fördert
gute Waldnutzung
FSC® C083411

Contents

Acknowledgements —— 1

Abbreviations —— 3

Original Publications —— 7

Introduction: My Way with Micah —— 9

Micah in the Low Countries —— 15

Micah in Neo-Assyrian Light —— 31

Religious Polemics in the Book of Micah —— 47

Das Gleichnis vom Frieden
Der Ort und die Funktion von Micha 4 in der Komposition des Buches
Micha —— 63

Israel and the Nations in the Book of Micah —— 71

'Who does not make firm his anger forever?'
Bodily Metaphors for YHWH in Micah 6–7 —— 81

That is Really Good: Remarks on Micah 6,8 —— 91

Gender Ambiguity in Micah 7:8–13 as a Reflection of Divine Gender
Notes on Micah 7:8–13 —— 103

Bien étonnés de se trouver ensemble
The Book of Micah and papyrus Amherst —— 115

Two Additions to DDD —— 131

Bibliography —— 135

Index of Modern Authors —— 149

Index of Sources —— 153

Index of Subjects —— 159

Acknowledgements

During the IOSOT meeting in Zürich, 2020, I had a pleasant conversation with Dr Albrecht Döhnert at the bookstand of the publishing company Walter de Gruyter. After discussing the tendencies in the world and especially the way Hebrew Bible scholarship was sailing, we talked about the proposal to edit a set of essays on the Biblical Book of Micah. My design for such a volume was soon accepted by the editorial board of BZAW for which I am thankful.

I would like to thank the staff at De Gruyter for the care they gave to my book. The various publishing houses and editorial boards of the volumes in which my work had previously been published kindly gave me their permission to reproduce my work in this volume. Special thanks go to Ove Kähler, managing director of Mohr/Siebeck, for his permission to reprint 'Das Gleichnis vom Frieden: Der Ort und die Funktion von Micha 4 in der Komposition des Buches Micha'; Mackenzie Brunnhuber, Penn State Press, for allowing to include Micah in Neo-Assyrian Light'; and Suzanne Mecking, Brill Publishing House, for her kind permission to reprint the three articles formerly edited by Brill: 'Micah in the Low Countries'; 'Religious Polemics in the Book of Micah'; and 'That is Really Good: Remarks on Micah 6,8'.

I did not alter the text of the previously published articles, except for a few typos and spelling errors.

https://doi.org/10.1515/9783111208657-001

Abbreviations

AAWG.PH	Abhandlungen der Akademie der Wissenschaften zu Göttingen, Philologisch-Historische Klasse
AB	Anchor Bible
AIIL	Ancient Israel and Its Literature
AOAT	Alter Orient und Altes Testament
AOS	American Oriental Studies
ASA	Association of Social Anthropologists
ASTI	*Annual of the Swedish Theological Institute*
ATANT	Abhandlungen zur Theologie des Alten und Neuen Testaments
ATD	das Alte Testament Deutsch
BBS	L. W. King, *Babylonian Boundary Stones and Memorial Tablets in the British Museum*, London 1912
BeO	Biblica et Orientalia
BEvTh	Beiträge zur Evangelische Theologie
BIN	Babylonian Inscriptions in the Collection of J. B. Nies
BiOr	*Bibliotheca Orientalis*
BIS	Biblical Interpretation Supplements
BiZs	*Biblisches Zeitschrift*
BKAT	Biblische Kommentar zum Alten Testament
BN	*Biblische Notizen*
BWANT	*Beiträge zur Wissenschaft vom Alten und Neuen Testament*
BZAW	Beihefte zur Zeitschrift für die Alttestamentliche Wissenschaft
CAD	Martha T. Roth (ed.), *The Assyrian Dictionary of the Oriental Institute of the University of Chicago*
CBS	*Tablets in the Collection of the University Museum of the University of Pennsylvania*
CBQ	*Catholic Biblical Quarterly*
CHANE	Culture and History of the Ancient Near East
ConB OT	Coniectanea Biblica, Old Testament Series
COS	*Context of Scripture*
CTB	Calwer Taschenbibliothek
DCH	*Dictionary of Classical Hebrew*
DDD	K. van der Toorn, B. Becking, P. W. van der Horst (eds), *Dictionary of Deities and Demons in the Bible: Second Extensivily Revised Edition*, Leiden-Grand Rapids-Cambridge UK 1999
DNWSI	J. Hoftijzer and K. Jongeling, *Dictionary of the North-West Semitic Inscriptions* (2 vols), Leiden 1995
ESV	English Standard Version
ETS	Evangelical Theological Society
FAT	Forschungen zum Alten Testament
FOTL	Forms of Old Testament Literature
FRLANT	*Forschungen zur Religion und Literatur des Alten und Neuen Testaments*
GAT	Grundrisse zum Alten Testament
HBM	Hebrew Bible Monographs
HCOT	Historical Commentary on the Old Testament
HSM	Harvard Semitic Museum

https://doi.org/10.1515/9783111208657-002

HThKAT	Herders Theologisches Kommentar zum Alten Testament
HTS	Hervormde Teologische Studies
IBT	Interpreting Biblical Texts
ICC	International Critical Commentary
JAB	*Journal for the Aramaic Bible*
JAOS	*Journal of the American Oriental Society*
JBL	*Journal of Biblical Literature*
JBQ	*Jewish Biblical Quarterly*
JCS	*Journal of Cuneiform Studies*
JEOL	*Jaarbericht Ex Oriente Lux*
JHS	*Journal for Hebrew Studies*
JNES	*Journal of Near Eastern Studies*
JNSL	*Journal of Northwest Semitic Languages*
JSOT	*Journal for the Study of the Old Testament*
JSOT Sup	Supplements to the Journal for the Study of the Old Testament
JSP Sup	Journal for the Study of Pseudepigrapha Supplement Series
KAI	H. Donner, O. Röllig, *Kanaanäische und Aramäische Inschriften*, Wiesbaden 1976
KAR	Keilschrifttexte aus Assur religiösen Inhalts
KJV	*King James Version*
KTU	M. Dietrich, O. Loretz, J. Sanmartín, *The Cuneiform alphabetic texts: from Ugarit, Ras Ibn Hani and other places (KTU)*, Münster 1995
LHB/OTS	Library of Hebrew Bible/Old Testament Studies
MT	Masoretic Text
NAS	New American Standard Bible
NTT	Nederlands Theologisch Tijdschrift
OBO	*Orbis Biblicus et Orientalis*
OTE	*Old Testament Essays*
OTL	Old Testament Literature
OTS	Oud Testamentische Studiën
PEQ	*Palestine Exploration Quarterly*
POT	de Prediking van het Oude Testament
RB	*Revue Biblique*
SAA	State Archives of Assyria
SAACT	State Archives of Assyria Cuneiform Texts
SAAS	State Archives of Assyria Studies
SBL DS	Society of Biblical Literature Dissertation Series
SBL WAW	Society of Biblical Literature Writings from the Ancient World
SBS	Stuttgarter Bibel Studien
SBT	Studies in Biblical Theology
SEÅ	*Svensk Exegetisk Årsbok*
SHCANE	Studies on the History and Culture of the Ancient Near East
SJOT	*Scandinavian Journal of the Old Testament*
SThAR	Studies in Theology and Religion
STVC	E. Chiera, *Sumerian Texts of Various Contents*, Chicago 1934
ThW	Theologische Wissenschaft
TRE	*Theologische Real Enzyklopädie*
UET	Ur Excavations, Texts

UM	*Tablets in the Collection of the University Museum of the University of Pennsylvania*
UF	Ugarit Forschungen
VAB	Vorderasiatische Bibliothek
VT	Vetus Testamentum
VTE	D. J. Wiseman, The Vassal Treaties of Esarhaddon, London 1958
VT Sup	Supplements to Vetus Testamentum
WBC	Word Biblical Commentary
WMANT	Wissenschaftliche Monographien zum Alten und Neuen Testament
YABRL	Yale Anchor Bible Reference Library
ZA	*Zeitschrift für Assyriologie und vorderasiatische Archäologie*
ZAbR	*Zeitschrift für Altorientalische und biblische Rechtsgeschichte*
ZAW	*Zeitschrift für die Alttestamentliche Wissenschaft*
ZDMG	*Zeitschrift der Deutschen Morgenländische Gesellschaft*
ZS	*Zeitschrift für Semitistik*

Original Publications

'Micah in the Low Countries', was first published in: K. Spronk (ed.), *The Present State of Old Testament Studies in the Low Countries* (OTS 69), Leiden 2016, pp. 13–29.

'Micah in Neo-Assyrian Light', was first published in: R. P. Gordon, H. M. Barstad (ed.), *"Thus speaks Ishtar of Arbela": Prophecy in Israel, Assyria, and Egypt in the Neo-Assyrian Period*, Winona Lake 2013, pp. 111–128.

'Religious Polemics in the Book of Micah', was first published in: R. L. Thelle, T. Stordalen and M. E. J. Richardson (eds), *New Perspectives on Old Testament Prophecy and History: Essays in Honour of Hans M. Barstad* (VT Sup 168), Leiden 2015, pp. 74–89.

'Das Gleichnis vom Frieden: Der Ort und die Funktion von Micha 4 in der Komposition des Buches Micha', was first published in: R. Müller, U. Nõmmik und J. Pakkala (eds), *Fortgeschriebenes Gotteswort Studien zu Geschichte, Theologie und Auslegung des Alten Testaments Festschrift für Christoph Levin zum 70. Geburtstag*, Tübingen 2020, pp. 309–16.

'Israel and the Nations in the Book of Micah' is a reworked paper presented at the SBL Annual Meeting, Atlanta 2010.

'Who does not make firm his anger forever?' Bodily Metaphors for YHWH in Micah 6–7' is a reworked paper presented at the EABS Meeting in Warsaw 2019.

'That is Really Good: Remarks on Micah 6,8', was first published in: A. Gow, P. Sabo (eds), *Tzedek, Tzedek Tsirtof: Poetry, Prophecy, and Justice in Hebrew Scripture: Essays in Honor of Francis Landy on the Occasion of his Seventieth Birthday* (Biblical Interpretation Series, 137), Leiden 2017, pp. 196–210.

'Gender Ambiguity in Micah 7:8–13 as a Reflection of Divine Gender: Notes on Micah 7:8–13' is newly written.

'Bien étonnés de se trouver ensemble: The Book of Micah and papyrus Amherst' is newly written.

'Biters and Breakers: Two Additions to *DDD*' is newly written.

https://doi.org/10.1515/9783111208657-003

Introduction: My Way with Micah

I cannot remember the first time I became aware of the prophetic book of Micah. Somewhere during my education at primary- and grammar school, I had to learn the concatenation of the twelve Minor Prophets by heart. To me as a schoolboy, this was a kind of knowledge not much different from the enumeration of the tributaries of the Danube. They were facts to take for granted that however had no influential relation with your personal life. At the age of – let us say – 15, I had no idea who the prophet Micah was or about the character of his message. I knew about Ecclesiastes 3, since the Byrds had turned the appropriation of that text by Pete Seeger into an immortal song 'Turn! Turn! Turn!'.[1]

This all changed during my time as a student of theology at Utrecht University in the 1970-ies. I discovered that the Book of Micah presented a message of uncompromising social justice: the poor should be helped and the rich needed to sing a little lower. In hindsight, I understand that the spirit of the times was of no little help to read this message in the prophetic text. In those days the Vietnam-war was coming to an end and their seemed to be a momentum for a third way between exploitative capitalism and dehumanizing communism. Micah, to me then was a voice in the choir longing for a socialism with a human face and a liberating faith. Many years later and wiser by the experiences of life, I have to admit that the human society and its economic fabric is more complex than I thought back then. Nevertheless, Micah still summons not to forget the bitter fate of all the *personae miserae* in the world.[2]

At the more exegetical level, I made another discovery – or better I became aware of a conceptual problem in the present text of the Book of Micah. Phrased as a question: How could a prophet announcing salvation and forthcoming peace, also utter bitter prospects of doom and decay. Just when I started to grasp the Wellhausian solution of this problem – the optimistic section were later added by a writer/redactor who was influenced by the prophecies of salvation to be found in Isaiah 40–66 – the commentary of Adam van der Woude on Micah appeared.[3] He had elaborated an ingenious theory to explain the alternation between the two types of prophecy.[4] In his opinion, Micah 2–5 contains the text of a dialogue between the pessimistic prophet Micah on the one hand and a group of optimistic pseudo-prophets on the other. Originally, I considered his insight as an ingenious solution that explained many features in Micah 2–5 and was ready

---

1 Rogan, *Byrds*; Valdez, "Folk Rock".
2 For comparable thoughts see O'Brien, *Micah*.
3 Wellhausen, *Kleine Propheten*, 142–43; Van der Woude, *Micha*.
4 Van der Woude, "Micah in Dispute"; Van der Woude, *Micha*, 61–192.

https://doi.org/10.1515/9783111208657-004

to adopt it. Over the years, some doubts slipped in. The assumed dispute is not marked by indicators such as 'I said'; 'they answered'; 'he refuted', or the like. This observation implies that even if there were a dispute, it has been veiled by a redactor. The language – in the sense of word-choice, grammatical constructions, and idiomatic expressions – does not differ between the two types of prophetic announcements. This implies that there is greater chance of a single authorship at least for chapters 2–5. The problem how to explain the alteration, however, remained. The solution by Wellhausen was blunt as well as one-dimensional in my view. I distrusted the presupposition that a prophet could only utter words and announcements in one dimensions.

In the meantime, I became a minister in the Dutch Reformed Church. In the hours for study I focused on the research that would lead to my dissertation on 2 Kings 17, defended at Utrecht University on 1985.[5] The interpretation of the Book of Micah slumbered in the backwoods of my thoughts, although occasionally I read a sermon on parts of the book. Micah 4 was an obvious choice for the 'Vredeszondag'.[6] These sermons culminated in a series of services transmitted on national radio and published in a small booklet.[7]

Around 1990 the *redaktionsgeschichtliche* approach was adopted by scholars working on the Book of the XII Minor Prophets. James Nogalski can be praised for being a pioneer in this approach. In his monographs he argued for the presence of similarly phrased little building blocks at the end of one prophetic book and at the beginning of the next. This phenomenon is then explained by a theory that starting in the exilic period the 'books' of the minor prophets were collected and connected by a redactor.[8] Ten years later a second wave of studies on the emergence and growing together of the Book of the XII Minor Prophets. This wave lead to a multitude of proposals that differed among each other. In the twenty-first century a third wave of the *redaktionsgeschichtliche* approach to the composition and emergence of the Book of the XII Minor Prophets arose. These studies propose an even more complicated redactional process behind the present textual form of the Dodekapropheton.[9] It should be noted that among the scholars favoring this approach there is no consensus with regard to the details of the process. In fact, Biblical scholars are presented a bewildering multitude of

---

5 Becking, *Ondergang*.
6 Each year in September the Dutch churches pay attention to the theme of peace and its absence in the present age.
7 Becking, *Dwarse dromer*.
8 Nogalski, *Literary Precursors*; Nogalski, *Redactional Processes*. See also Schart, *Entstehung*.
9 See, e.g., Wöhrle, *Frühen Sammlungen*; Wöhrle, *Abschluss*; Hagedorn, *Anderen im Spiegel*; Zapff, "Book of Micah"; LeCureux, *Thematic Unity*.

opinions which makes the functionality of this approach questionable. As for the problem of the alteration of doom and salvation in Micah 2–5, the *redaktionsgeschichtliche* approach lead to proposals that make them fifth generation grandchildren of Wellhausen. Both dimensions of prophecy are seen as stemming from different redactors.

When I was working on my monograph on Jeremiah 30–31,[10] Karel van der Toorn hinted me at the Mesopotamian proto-apocalyptic prophecies as text that show an alteration between 'good times and bad times'.[11] The underlying approach to history in these texts helped me to understand Jeremiah's book of consolation as an announcement of a two stage futurology. In these chapters I detected references to two transformations. The first one was looking back into Israel's past and evaluated the conquest of Jerusalem and the subsequent Babylonian exile as punishment by YHWH for Israel's and Judah's transgressions. The second transformation was looking into the impending future that would contain the effects of God's grace: the end of the exile, the return to the promised land, and life under a new relationship.

Since this pattern helped in clarifying the textual dynamics of Jeremiah 30–31, I had hope that it could be helpful for Micha 2–5 as well. I tested this assumption in two articles – both reproduced in this volume. As a result, I was able to propose construing Micha 2–5 as the expression of a two-staged futurology: the impending doom would eventually, 'in the end of the days', be redeemed by salvation rooted in divine grace.[12]

During one of the Annual Meetings of the Society of Biblical Studies, I had a nice conversation with John Collins. He is an internationally acknowledged and esteemed scholar who had taken over the responsibilities as general editor of the Anchor Bible, now renamed Anchor Yale Bible. He was probing the field for authors of commentaries in this prestigious series or of one of the accompanying volumes in the Anchor Yale Bible Reference Library. At the end of our talk, I accepted the invitation to write a commentary on the Book of Micah as a replacement of the existing work of Francis Andersen and Noel Freedman.[13] This coerced me to study the Book of Micah in all its details and to formulate proposals as to the many problems the reading of this text provokes in a coherent way. It took me a few years – more than I anticipated – to finish this book. Despite the many sometimes dull hours at my desk, I am still of the opinion that the Book of Micah contains a test that is relevant even for our times full of crisis.

---

10 Becking, *Between Fear and Freedom*.
11 See Longman, *Fictional Akkadian Autobiography*.
12 Becking, "Exile does not Equal the Eschaton"; Becking, "Micah in Neo-Assyrian Light".
13 Andersen and D. N. Freedman, *Micah*.

The essays in this volume reflect my trajectory with the Book of Micah. 'Micah in the Low Countries' sketches the development of Dutch research on the Book of Micah during the sixty years after the end of World War II. There is a clear tendency detectable in the character of these studies. In the early years research stood in the service of the church(es) and of (Christian) education. The horizon was mainly national. Publications from beyond the border were quoted, but the vast majority of the own publications were in Dutch. Around 1960 there is a clear move towards the international audience. Adam van der Woude played an important role in this process. Nowadays, publications by Dutch scholars are seldomly written in our mother's tongue. The development in the Low Countries runs mainly parallel to the international current with two exceptions. (1) The *redaktionsgeschichtliche* approach did no gain solid ground in Belgium and the Netherlands. (2) The attention for a poetical analysis using the unit delimiters in ancient manuscript is a typical Dutch preponderance.

'Micah in Neo-Assyrian Light' offers an assessment Mesopotamian parallels to the Book of Micah. The parallels are to be found at three levels: (a) Words and phrases; (b) Idiomatic expressions; and (c) Conceptual designs. Especially the third category is of importance for my idea of the presence of a two staged futurology in the Book of Micah.

'Religious Polemics in the Book of Micah' discusses the view(s) of the author(s) of the Book of Micah with respect to other religions and to other forms of Yahwism. An analysis of the evidence makes clear that the author(s) do not advocate a strictly monotheistic form of Yahwism. The existence of other deities is not negated, but they are incomparable to Yhwh. As for the other forms of Yahwism, the author(s) vehemently contest forms of Yahwism that are connected with idols or lead to the oppression of the *personae miserae*.

'The Exile does not Equal the Eschaton: An Interpretation of Micah 4:1–5', offers an analysis of the famous words in Micah 4 on the forthcoming peace. I argue that the view of Adam van der Woude who assumes that the pseudo-prophets are quoting Isaiah 2 in order to counter Micah's prophecy of doom in Micah 3, is untenable. The unit represents the second stage of the two staged futurology in Micah 2–5.

'Das Gleichnis vom Frieden: Der Ort und die Funktion von Micha 4 in der Komposition des Buches Micha' continues on the previous essay. I here connect the text from Micah with passages from Jeremiah 22 and the prayer of Solomon. Next to that, I read Mic. 4:1–4 in connection with the end of Micah 3. The parable on peace should be construed as a transformation of a tradition about the peoples looking at the dire fate of Israel while adding an element of hope. Since the elements of this tradition are found in Mi 3:9–4:5 but not in Isa 2:2–5, it is more likely that the author of Isa 2–12 took the parable from Micah.

'Israel and the Nations in the Book of Micah' investigates the role that Israel, the Nations, and the interaction between the two plays in the Book of Micah. Interestingly, this role differs in the various parts of the Book of Micah. The differences can be clarified by assuming redaction-historical division into three sections: Micah 1; 2–5; 6–7. The middle part of the book is seen as a prophetic futurology that talks about two different futures: an immanent and more eschatological. The authors of this book are mostly concerned with the fate of Israel. The nations do not play the main part, but they act or will act in the various roles as instruments of the divine love for this specific nation. Even in the prophecies of doom God is to be seen as acting on behalf of the real interest of Israel.

'Who does not make firm his anger forever?' Bodily Metaphors for YHWH in Micah 6–7' investigates the suggestion made by Juan Cruz. In his view the literary unity of the Book of Micah can be substantiated by a look at the use of metaphors made throughout the book. He claims that the legal and pastoral metaphors in Micah 1–5 function in the same way as they do in chapters 6–7. A closer look at the evidence, however, makes clear that his view is untenable.

'That is Really Good: Remarks on Micah 6,8' discusses the translation of the famous moral impetus in Micah 6. As rendition of the final line, 'and to act deliberately by walking with your God' is proposed. As a *Gebot der Stunde* is construed as being of great importance for a world that seems to have lost its moral compass.

'Gender Ambiguity in Micah 7:8–13 as a Reflection of Divine Gender: Notes on Micah 7:8–13' starts with the observation that the word *ᵓelōhāyik*, "your God", has a feminine suffix, implying that the prophetic "I" figure in this unit was construed as a woman. This observation is connected with the phenomenon of gender-ambiguity of spokespersons in some Neo-Assyrian prophetic texts and the unclear gender of the deity Ishtar in whose name these prophets spoke. This leads to the question whether Micha and his God also should be seen as having a gender-ambiguity.

'Bien étonnés de se trouver ensemble: The Book of Micah and papyrus Amherst' discusses a possible parallel between the until recently enigmatic text of the Aramaic inscription in Demotic script and the Book of Micah. There are no parallels at the level of prophetic formula. The 'fear not' introduction is absent in Micah, while the 'woe-oracle' has no counterpart in Papyrus Amherst 63. Both texts, however, contain a hymnic unit on divine incomparability. It is important to note that such a text, generally seen as a sign of a monotheistic religion, is present in a text with a clear polytheistic fabric.

'Biters and Breakers: Two Additions to *DDD*'. In the *Dictionary of Deities and Demons in the Hebrew Bible*, are included so called demythologized deities, i.e. Hebrew or Greek nouns that as such refer to a divine being in other cultures, for example 'Sun'. My reading of Micah 5:4 revealed that two items should have been included: Biters נסיכים, and Breakers רעים. The present essay repairs this omission.

It has been a pleasure for me to delve into the depths of the Book of Micah. I hope that this collection shows some of this joy.

Micah in the Low Countries

Long before critical scholarship, the prophet Micah was already known in the Low Countries. In a closed part of the retable 'Agnus Dei' Jan van Eyck painted in 1432 the prophet empathically looking downwards to the virgin Mary.[1] This scene is probably inspired by the reference to Micah in the nativity narrative of Matthew. With the rise of critical scholarship, the prophets were slowly alienated from their forecasting-messianic role and read in the framework of their own time.[2] I will confine myself to the scholarly work on Micah written by scholars from the Low Countries since the Second World War.[3]

1 Starting Point: Vriezen 1948

Although Micah is only one of twelve minor prophets about whom books have been collected in the Hebrew Bible, the scholarly movements around the seven chapters of this Biblical book are exemplary for research in the Low Countries on the *Dodekapropheton* in the post-World War II era. I start my inquiries with the textbook that Theodoor Vriezen published in 1947.[4] In this Introduction Vriezen dedicates some four pages to his views on the Book of Micah.[5] He dates the prophet and the core of the book to the second half of the eighth century BCE. According to him, only a few lines in chapter 7 are not authentic. He construes Micah to be a pupil of Isaiah. Micah adopted the famous vision of the forthcoming realm of peace (Mic. 4:2–5) from his Jerusalemite master (Isa. 2). Vriezen sees two highlights in the text of Micah: the prophecy of doom for the temple in 3:12 and the words on the true character of religion (Mic. 6:8). As elsewhere in this

---

1 See Philip, *Ghent altarpiece*; De Vos, *Vlaamse Primitieven*, Picture 47.
2 See for the Low Countries De Vries, *Bible and Theology*.
3 Publications for a more general audience are not included; see, e.g., Grollenberg, "Micha 7"; Deurloo en Van Woerden, *Om het recht lief te hebben*; Van der Woude, *Profeet en establishment*; Schuman, *Micha*; Becking, *Dwarse dromer*.
4 Vriezen, *Geschriften*. The book was later republished under a different title: Vriezen, *Literatuur*; a thoroughly reworked version appeared in 1973 (Vriezen en Van der Woude, *Literatuur*; Katwijk ⁶1980), in which Adam Van der Woude wrote the sections on the deuterocanonical and pseudepigraphic books; after Vriezen's death, Adam Van der Woude prepared a completely new edition, that after Van der Woude's death has been published by Ed Noort in cooperation with Fiorentino García Martínez: Vriezen en Van der Woude, *Oudisraelitische en vroegjoodse*, a few years later an English edition saw the light: Vriezen and Van der Woude, *Literature*. Over the years the book has been updated, but the basic frame remained.
5 Vriezen, *Geschriften*, 185–188.

https://doi.org/10.1515/9783111208657-005

introduction, Vriezen assesses the prophet Micah by a nineteenth century liberal protestant concept of prophecy. Prophets were individuals who were enlightened by the true moral religion. It is interesting to note that Vriezen does not make any remark on the interrelationship between the prophecies of doom and the prophecies of salvation in the Book of Micah. All in all, his view is rather characteristic for his time and his position.

By today's standards his views are slightly obsolete. In the next sections, I will try to sketch how research by Dutch and Flemish scholars was instrumental in the change of view on Micah.

2 Fifties and Sixties: The Calm before the Storm

In the period up to the end of the nineteen-sixties not much research was done on the Book of Micah. A few commentaries appeared two written by protestant[6] and two by catholic scholars.[7] These commentaries have in general a pious character. They are designed to help preachers in preparing a sermon, but could also be of help in bible-study groups. I will not discuss all four of them but focus on the commentary written by Edelkoort which, in my view, is exemplary for the all four. Before his appointment as ordinarius for Old Testament study at Utrecht University in 1945, Edelkoort had served the Dutch Reformed Church as a minister in various communities.[8]

In his – at times long-winded – commentary, he defends the position that a greater part of the present book of Micah was written by the prophet himself. Later readers added only two sections: (1) the vision of the forthcoming realm of peace in Micah 4 had been incorporated by readers who were looking for a touch of salvation amidst the prophecies of doom and (2) the final section Micah 7:7–20 that was added in the Babylonian Exile. Edelkoort immediately hurries to state that non-authenticity would not implicate a loss of value, since these added sections are written in the same Divine Spirit that breathes through the whole of Scripture.[9] He argues that Isaiah 2 must have been the source for Micah 4 and not the other way around. His main argument is not linguistic, but conceptual. It is inconceivable that the great Isaiah, the Prince of all prophets, would have borrowed a text from a person who came from the periphery of Israelite society.[10]

---

6 Edelkoort, *Micha*; Ridderbos, *Kleine profeten II*.

7 Coppens, *Douze petits prophètes*; Deden, *Kleine profeten*.

8 For biographical details see De Groot, "Edelkoort".

9 Edelkoort, *Micha*, 16.

10 Edelkoort, *Micha*, 16; this view is drenched in a bourgeois ideology that prefers city life over the countryside, a view that has been challenged by Wolff, "Micah the Moreshite".

It is of great interest to note that Edelkoort has given some interpretations that can be seen as the prototype of the later 'discussion-thesis' elaborated by Adam van der Woude. Edelkoort notes an antithesis between Micah and a group of prophets that are very much in favour of the politics of the then ruling class. Edelkoort construes the present text of the Book of Micah as containing sections in which the words of the 'other prophets' are given voice, as for instance in Micah 2:6–11.[11] There is another incentive in his work. Confronted with the problem how to conceptually combine the two types of prophecies in Micah 2–5 – doom and salvation – he proposes a two-stage futurology. In the short run there will be doom for Israel – as a punishment for its sins – but in a later future there will be salvation, based on divine grace.[12]

Although Edelkoort reads the Messiah in the famous text from Micah 5 on Bethlehem, he meanders between three positions: (1) the text would refer to the contemporary situation of the prophet in the eighth century BCE; (2) the text shows light on the life and time of Jesus the Messiah from Nazareth and (3) the text should be read in light of the Second Coming of Christ.[13] Although the inclusion of the first position was a brave act in those days, Edelkoort offers a lengthy and unclear balancing act between the confession of the Church and his personal scholarly insights.

Finally, Edelkoort construes the message of Micah as a reproach to ancient Israel on two fronts. On the one hand, the Israelites had sinned against God by accepting non-Mosaic forms of religion and on the other hand the elite of the country had forsaken the duties from Israel's social code towards the *personae miserae* of the society: women, widows and the poor.

The commentary by Edelkoort – as well as the other three mentioned above – has been influential in the Low Countries for quite some time. This is apparent for instance by designs for sermons in the homiletic yearbook *Postille* that was often consulted by ministers from the mainstream of the Reformed Churches.[14]

3 Dispute and Discussion: Adam van der Woude

Around 1960 plans were made for a new series of Dutch commentaries on the Hebrew Bible. This series *de Prediking van het Oude Testament* was designed to

---

11 Edelkoort, *Micha*, 16; see also his more scholarly article Edelkoort, "Prophet and Prophets".
12 See, e.g., Edelkoort, *Micha*, 52–57.
13 See also his more well-known work Edelkoort, *Christusverwachting* (The Expectation of Christ in the Old Testament).
14 See, e.g., the design draft for sermons on Micah 5:1f. by J. E. Uitman in *Postille* 13 (1961–62), 43–46; and on Micah 6:6–8 by C. van Leeuwen in *Postille* 15 (1953–64), 136–140.

be informative and scholarly based with an open eye for the fact that ministers had to preach. In general, the Hebrew Bible was no longer seen as just a *preparatio evangelicae*. The various authors were invited to explain the texts in their original historical and cultural settings. Systematic preoccupations are not supposed to rule over the exegetical enterprise.[15] Adam van der Woude was invited to write the volume on Micah. He more than once pointed out that during his preparatory research the Book of Micah was an impenetrable riddle to him. The text contained a set of enigmatic problems and it took Van der Woude a few years to untie the knots. Around 1970 he published a series of articles on the interpretation of the Book of Micah unfolding his views that are basic to his commentary and which will be discussed in the next three sections. It should be noted that Van der Woude, much more than scholars from the generation before him, was in constant discussion with scholars from all over the world.

3.1 A Geographically Ordered Prophecy of Doom

Van der Woude's view on Micah 1 is rather traditional although it deviates from the exegetical tradition around 1970. By then the majority of scholars construed Micah 1 to be composed out of two originally independent prophetic texts. Micah 1:2–7 was seen as a prophecy of doom delivered before the fall of Samaria, while Micah 1:8–16 was seen as connected with the events around Sennacherib's campaign in 701.[16] According to Van der Woude, Micah 1 should be construed as a literary unit. He interprets the chapter as rooted in a prophecy of doom spoken by the prophet in the precinct of Lachish in the period before the fall of Samaria. Although he detects various literary genres in the chapter, this difference in *Gattung* is not a signal for a literary critical division. The various parts of the chapter – theophany, prophecy of doom, wordplays on place names – are bound by a more general concept. Van der Woude construes Micah 1 as composed on the strategy of surprise. The text starts with a theophany that traditionally would lead to a verdict of guilty to the address of the other nations. Surprisingly, the first nation mentioned is the Northern Kingdom of Israel. Targeting the northerners, however, would have pleased the inhabitants of the Southern Kingdom of Judah. The next target of the prophecy of doom is Jerusalem, which would have pleased the inhabitants of Lachish, since to them Jerusalem was a chiffre of a wicked and

---

15 See also the introduction to the series by A. van Selms and A. S. van der Woude in the first volume that appeared: Van Selms, *Genesis I.*
16 See, e.g., Fohrer, „Micha 1".

evil city. Eventually, the prophecy of doom turns to Lachish and surrounding, surprising the audience.[17]

3.2 A Dispute with Pseudo-Prophets

The second part of the Book of Micah, chapters 2–5, is well known for its conceptual and compositional problems. In these chapters an interplay between prophecies of doom and prophecies of salvation can be found, as will be explained with the help of the following example. The vision of peace in Mic 4:1–4 is an example of the beauty of Hebrew poetry that is almost impossible to render in a translation:

> [1] But in the last days it shall come to pass, *that* the mountain of the house of the LORD shall be established in the top of the mountains, and it shall be exalted above the hills; and people shall flow unto it.
>
> [2] And many nations shall come, and say, Come, and let us go up to the mountain of the LORD, and to the house of the God of Jacob; and he will teach us of his ways, and we will walk in his paths: for the law shall go forth of Zion, and the word of the LORD from Jerusalem.
>
> [3] And he shall judge among many people, and rebuke strong nations afar off; and they shall beat their swords into plowshares, and their spears into pruninghooks: nation shall not lift up a sword against nation, neither shall they learn war any more.
>
> [4] But they shall sit every man under his vine and under his fig tree; and none shall make *them* afraid: for the mouth of the LORD of hosts hath spoken *it.*[18]

One of the main problems in the interpretation of Micah 2–5 comes to the fore when comparing these beautiful lines of hope with the final words of the previous chapter. Micah 3:12 contains a fierce prophecy of doom:

> Zion will be ploughed like a field,
>> Jerusalem will become a pile of ruins.

Micah 4:1–4 is a vision full of hope with tones of peace and welfare. Micah 3:12 can be seen as an example of the end of time, foreshadowing doom and anxiety; here the exile equals the eschaton, while Mic 4:1–4 is written in the language of a consoling perspective of a salvific eschaton. This is just one example of the

---

17 Van der Woude, "Micha 1:10–16"; Van der Woude, *Micha,* 19–22.
18 Micah 4:1–4, KJV.

enigmatic alternation of the themes of "hope" and "doom" in Micah. This inter-change has been interpreted in different ways.

The classical, nineteenth-century exegesis and its aftermath have constructed a literary-critical or redaction-historical solution, as has been done for various other places in the prophets where the same problem occurs. Wellhausen has characterized this redaction in his dictum that these later additions offered "Rosen und Lavendel statt Blut und Eisen."[19] In this view, Micah is seen as an eighth-century prophet of doom – compare Jeremiah 26 – but during or after the Babylonian exile the traditions relating to this prophet were augmented with optimistic phrases borrowed from the school of Deutero-Isaiah.[20] Other scholars had read Micah, or at least Micah 2–5 as a coherent text.[21]

Van der Woude elaborated an ingenious theory.[22] In his opinion, Micah 2–5 contains the text of a dialogue between the pessimistic prophet and some optimis-tic pseudo-prophets. As is well known, there are striking similarities between this text in Micah 4 and Isaiah 2. The scholarly discussion on this point had not reached a consensus around 1970, although there was a preference to see the Isianic version as authentic. Van der Woude presented the view that the optimis-tic opponents of Micah are quoting Isaiah as an objection against Micah's prophe-cy of doom. Their argument would have been: You might prophesy doom and exile; the great prophet Isaiah, however, has already said something else.[23] Van der Woude's view is attractive to some degree, especially since he is pointing to a very early example of abusing Scripture by quoting it literarily. Next to that his proposal is coherent with his solution of the 'doom'- 'salvation' dichotomy in Micah 2–5. Although his view has been adopted by some,[24] later scholarship abroad as well as in the Low Countries has challenged his position.

3.3 A Northern Micah

Very intriguing is Van der Woude's view on Micah 6–7. It has long been noticed that the language and the theology of the final two chapters of the Book of Micah

---

19 Wellhausen, *Kleine Propheten*, 96.
20 Wellhausen, *Kleine Propheten*, 142–43. See also, from the era before Van der Woude's publica-tions on Micah, Jeremias, „Deutung".
21 E.g., the more traditional Dutch commentaries mentioned above.
22 Van der Woude, "Micah in Dispute"; Van der Woude, *Micha*, 61–192.
23 Van der Woude, "Micah in Dispute"; Van der Woude, "Micah IV 1–5"; Van der Woude, *Micha*, 125–32.
24 In the later editions of Vriezen's introduction (see note 1); by Boogaart, *Reflections on Restora-tion*, 49–88; Strydom, *Micah*, 127–57; and by the Frisian translation of the Bible: *Nije Fryske*

differ from the preceding ones. Vriezen, for instance, hinted at some parallelisms between Micha 6–7 and the Book of Hosea – a northern prophet.[25] This observation had led to two positions regarding the emergence of Micah 6–7. Some scholars ascribed (parts of) Micah 6:1–7:7 to the author of Micah 1–5.[26] Others argue that the two chapters were added to the Micah-corpus in exilic or post-exilic times.[27]

Van der Woude opts for a different solution. In his view, Micah 6–7 was written by a prophet by the name of Micah. This Deutero-Micah prophesied in the Northern Kingdom about ten years before Micah of Moreshet-Gad.[28] The message of this prophet concurs with that of other Northern Prophets and with the proto-deuternonomistic theology. Religious and social trespasses are vehemently condemned. At the same time the more homiletic side of the text offer sign of hope to be given by the God of election and covenant. In fact, Van der Woude is reviving an old exegetical tradition. Earlier, scholars like Burkitt, Eissfeldt, and Willis had uttered comparable thoughts.[29] Van der Woude, however, substantiates this position by a range of seven arguments. Van der Woude's view on Micah 6–7 have not been taken over by many scholars. This might be due to the fact that relatively soon after the completion of his commentary, the *redaktionsgeschichtliche Welle* with a focus on the emergence of the *Dodekapropheton* as one book became dominant.

4 A Numerological Analysis: Cas Labuschagne

Cas Labuschagne – who worked together with Adam van der Woude in Groningen – is of the opinion that Biblical texts are based on numerological structures.[30] Texts are built in blocks of mainly 17 or 26 words. Labuschagne also looks at the distribution of words in verses before and after the *atnaḥ*, in main clauses and subordinated clauses, in narrative and direct speech. In his calculations he often comes across the numbers that in Jewish tradition stand for the holy name of God.

Bibeloersetting; Van der Woude was born in the Dutch province of Fryslan and was on the advisory board for this translation.

25 For instance by Th.C. Vriezen in Vriezen en Van der Woude, *Literatuur*, 250.

26 E.g., Jeremias, "Deutung", 330–354; Vriezen en Van der Woude, *Literatuur*, 250–52.

27 E.g., Th. Lescow, "Analyse", 182–212; Willi-Plein, *Vorformen*, 178.

28 Van der Woude, "Deutero Micha"; Van der Woude, *Micha* 195–99.

29 Burkitt, "Micah 6 and 7"; Eissfeldt, "Psalm"; Willis, "Hope Oracle".

30 For an introduction see Labuschagne, *Numerical Secrets*.

As for the Book of Micah, Labuschagne published an article that is often overlooked on the numerological composition of this prophetic book.[31] He detects a *menorah*-structure in the Book of Micah with chapter 4 as its centre. The unit Micah 4:11–14 contains 51 words, which is three times 17. The result of the analysis of other units does not fit that smoothly with Labuschagne's ideas. Although his work has not found wide recognition or acceptance, his approach is unique and remarkable.

5 Wellhausen Redivivus: Jan A. Wagenaar

In 2001, Jan Wagenaar published a revision of his hitherto unpublished Utrecht dissertation on the composition of Micah 2–5.[32] In this work he tackles the problem of the enigmatic alternation of the themes of "hope" and "doom" in Micah. This interchange has been interpreted in different ways which are presented in Wagenaar's *status questionis*.[33]

The classical, nineteenth-century exegesis and its aftermath have constructed a literary-critical or redaction-historical solution, as has been done for various other places in the prophets where the same problem occurs. Wellhausen has characterized this redaction in his dictum that these later additions offered "Rosen und Lavendel statt Blut und Eisen."[34] In this view, Micah is seen as an eighth-century prophet of doom – compare Jeremiah 26 – but during or after the Babylonian exile the traditions relating to this prophet were augmented with optimistic phrases borrowed from the school of Deutero-Isaiah.[35]

Other scholars read Micah, or at least Micah 2–5 as a coherent text.[36] According to Wagenaar this approach fails in coherently explaining the fissures in Micah 2–5. The third position – Van der Woude's dialogue model – has been displayed above.[37] This model, too, is assessed by Wagenaar as containing a set of flaws and misinterpretations.

---

31 Labuschagne, "Compositietechnieken". This publication is missing in the otherwise abundant bibliography in Andersen and Freedman, *Micah*.

32 Wagenaar, *Judgment and Salvation*; the Dutch original was only available in a limited edition: *Oordeel en heil*.

33 Wagenaar, *Judgment and Salvation*, 6–45. In the next footnotes I will only refer to publications that were available before Wagenaar's monograph.

34 Wellhausen, *Kleine Propheten*, 96.

35 Wellhausen, *Kleine Propheten* 142–43. This view was adopted by, e.g., Jeremias, "Deutung"; Mays, *Micah*; Collins, *Mantle*, 72–73; McKane, *Book*, 17–19; Kessler, *Micha*, 41–47.

36 E.g., Hagstrom, *Coherence*; Utzschneider, *Michas Reise*, 152–64; Dempsey, "Micah 2–3"; Wood, "Speech".

37 See 3.2.

After the introduction, Wagenaar presents a fresh translation of Micah 2–5. This translation is sustained by a meticulously thorough philological commentary in which the author shows his grammatical expertise and his ability to argue with the versions.[38] This section is full of detailed exegetical trouvailles of which I will only give two examples. He convincingly argues that the traditional rendition of the noun *'et* 'ploughshare' is inadequate. A translation of *'et* with 'hoe' is much more appropriate.[39] Elaborating on a suggestion made by Kevin Cathcart,[40] Wagenaar proposes to vocalise the word *r'ym* in Mic. 5:4 (ET 5) not as *ro'îm*, but as *rā'îm* and translate with 'we will raise against him seven evils (spirits), which is appropriate in the literary context and in accord with the idea expressed in Assyrian incantations in which seven demons were stirred up against invaders.[41]

In his final chapter, Wagenaar offers a very detailed literary-critical analysis of Micah 2–5.[42] In his reading of the various sub-units two methods go hand in hand, since he combines the traditional *Literarkritik* with a keen eye form form-critical observations. He arrives at the following conclusions.[43] The first draft of Micah 2–5 was composed in late pre-exilic times by disciples of the prophet. They produced the core of Micah 2–3, mainly the prophecies of doom. Circles around Jeremiah added in early exilic times a few elements in 2–3 and enlarged the composition with 4:9–10.14 and 5:9–13. In late exilic times writers from the school of Ezekiel added 2:12; 3:8*; 4:6–7a.8 and 5:1–4a. The first layer containing elements of hope were added by Isaianic circles in the early post-exilic age (esp. 4:1–5). With a few later glosses and the insertion of Micah 1; 6–7 the composition was completed in the Persian Period. This implies that the present Book of Micah should be seen as the final product of a complex redaction-historical process. In line with Wellhausen, Wagenaar offers a solution of the problem of the enigmatic alternation of the themes of "hope" and "doom" in Micah, he, however, fails in arguing why these elements of hope were included at exactly where they now stand.

6 A helpful tool: Adri van der Wal

When the Personal Computer reached the scholarly world of humanities around 1980, Eep Talstra working at the Free University of Amsterdam was visionary

---

38 Wagenaar, *Judgment and Salvation*, 49–201.
39 See Wagenaar, *Judgment and Salvation*, 138–39.
40 Cathcart, "Notes".
41 Wagenaar, *Judgment and Salvation*, 183–84.
42 Wagenaar, *Judgment and Salvation*, 202–315.
43 See the survey: Wagenaar, *Judgment and Salvation*, 327–28.

with regard to the application of this technology for Biblical Studies. This is not the place to write the history of what now is the 'Eep Talstra Centre for Bible and Computer'. In the framework of this article, I will only refer to an early fruit of this research. In 1990 Adri van der Wal published a valuable bibliographical tool prepared with assistance of a computer. He collected and selected all relevant publications on the Book of Micah.[44] With the present strong search engines on the internet, bibliographical features can all too easily be connected. 25 years ago, tools like Van der Wal's bibliography were welcomed as an important step forward.

7 Die Redaktionsgeschichtliche Welle or the Role of Micah in the Growth of the *Dodekapropheton*

The *redaktionsgeschichtliche* research on Biblical texts started in 1956 with the publication by Willi Marxsen of his book on Mark as author of the gospel.[45] It took a few years before the method became an accepted tool in Old Testament scholarship.[46] The method aims at analysing the various redactional stages of a composition looking for the way in which the redactor reapplied existing traditions to a changed situation. One of the first important fruits on this new branch of scholarship was the analysis by Walter Dietrich of the redactional growth of the Book of Kings.[47]

Around 1990 the method was adopted by scholars working on the Book of the XII Minor Prophets. James Nogalski can be praised for being a pioneer in this approach. In his monographs he argued for the presence of similarly phrased little building blocks at the end of one prophetic book and at the beginning of the next. This phenomenon is then explained by a theory that starting in the exilic period the 'books' of the minor prophets were collected and redactionally connected.[48] Ten years later a second wave of studies on the emergence and growing together of the Book of the XII Minor Prophets. It is not within the aim of this article to describe the developments in this area of research in full detail.

In the twenty-first century a third wave of the *redaktionsgeschichtliche* approach to the composition and emergence of the Book of the XII Minor Prophets arose. These studies propose an even more complicated redactional process be-

---

44 Van der Wal, *Micah*.

45 Marxsen, *Evangelist Markus*.

46 See Kratz und Merk, "Redaktionsgeschichte/Redaktionskritik".

47 Dietrich, *Prophetie und Geschichte*.

48 Nogalski, *Literary Precursors*; Nogalski, *Redactional Processes*. See also Schart, *Entstehung*.

hind the present textual form of the Dodekapropheton. This is not the place to discuss all these proposals in detail.[49]

It is remarkable that this branch of research did not find many echoes in studies on Micah from the Low Countries. There are only two publications to be mentioned here. In an interesting article, Stefan Paas made the following observations.[50] He remarks that in recent research a consensus seems to have been reached regarding the redactional and theological unity of the Dodekapropheton. Despite weaker points in the arguments and some forms of criticism – especially on the specificity of the prophetic Books under consideration – the *redaktionsgeschichtliche* thesis is construed as self-evident by its adherers. Paas argues that if the thesis were correct, then thematic and verbal relations between the beginning of the Dodekapropheton must be detectable. He then discusses three possibilities – divine love; divine creation and the marriage metaphor – and concludes that the basic redactional unity of the Dodekapropheton is far from self-evident. Paas does not pay much attention to the Book of Micah. Next to that, it would be interesting whether his argument could stand upright after the second more sophisticated wave of the *redaktionsgeschichtliche* approach. In his dissertation defended at the Radboud University in Nijmegen, C. F. M. van den Hout focuses on the Book of Zechariah. He presents a mild form of criticism towards the *redaktionsgeschichtliche* approach, but he does not refer to the Book of Micah.[51]

8 Cantos and Cola: Johannes C. de Moor

In studies of and commentaries on the Book of Micah the division of the textual units is often haphazard. A division between all these units is often made on the basis of the – supposed – contents. Adam van der Woude delimitates the paragraphs in Micah 2–5 according to the two voices he has detected in the dialogue.[52] Cas Labuschagne supposes that a careful numerological analysis will lead to the correct division of the smaller units within the *menorah*-structure.[53] Jan Wagenaar organizes the building blocks of the composition according to the various *Gattungen* he supposed to be present in Micah.[54] Such approaches lead to the absence of a consensus regarding the delimitation of the Book of Micah.

---

49 See, e.g., Wöhrle, *Frühen Sammlungen*; Wöhrle, *Abschluss*; Hagedorn, *Anderen im Spiegel*; Zapff, "Book of Micah"; LeCureux, *Thematic Unity*.
50 Paas, "Bookends Themes".
51 Van den Hout, *Struikelblokken*.
52 Van der Woude, *Micha*, 61–192.
53 Labuschagne, 'Opmerkelijke compositietechnieken'.
54 Wagenaar, *Judgment and Salvation*.

In 1979 Josef Oesch published a ground-breaking monograph on an until then under-exposed feature of the Masoretic Text of the Hebrew Bible.[55] Oesch collected the data on the *Petuchot* and *Setumot* presenting them as the reflections of an age old system of paragraphing the text of the Hebrew Bible. Some twenty years later the *Pericope*-group reformulated his work in a new research strategy. This group – with Marjo Korpel as its pivot – is collecting data from ancient manuscripts (mainly Hebrew, Greek, Syriac, Latin) on the delimitation of the Books of the Bible. In doing so, a more firm basis for the division into textual units is hoped to be found.

In the frame-work of this project, Johannes de Moor has published a set of articles on the Book of Micah.[56] In these essays he reached a series of interesting results of which I will only mention a few.

In one of these articles, De Moor addresses the often debated issue of the proper subdivision of Micah 2:1–13.[57] On the basis of the analysis of more than 100 ancient Hebrew manuscripts, along with a smaller number of manuscripts from several major ancient versions De Moor arrives at a new understanding of the colometry as well as of the paragraphing of Micah 2. As for the colometry, he states that the manuscript evidence indicates that the colometric text divisions in the Masoretic text are to be preferred.[58] As for its units, Micah 2 can best be delimitated into three sub-canto's: Micah 2:1–5; 6–11; 12–13.[59] I will give a graphic representation of his findings:

The Structure of Micah 2		
Sub-canto's	**Canticles**	**Strophes**
A: 1–5	A.i 1–2	A.i.1 1
		A.I.2 2
	A.i 3	A.ii.1 3
	A.iii 4–5	A.iii.1 4
		A.iii.2 5

---

55 Oesch, *Petucha und Setuma*.
56 J. C. de Moor is emeritus professor for Semitic Languages of the – no longer existing – Theological University at Kampen. He supervised the dissertation of Marjo Korpel and published together with her *The Structure of Classical Hebrew Poetry*. The book can be seen as a way-station between the monograph of Oesch and the work of the Pericope group. On Micah, de Moor published: De Moor, "Unit Division"; "Micah 7: 1–13"; "Micah 2: 1–13"; "Micah 6".
57 De Moor, "Micah 2: 1–13".
58 De Moor, "Micah 2: 1–13", 99.
59 De Moor, "The Structure of Micah 2: 1–13", 99–101.

(continued)

The Structure of Micah 2

Sub-canto's	Canticles	Strophes	
B: 6–11	B.i 6–7	B.i.1	6
		B.i.2	7
	B.ii 8–9	B.ii.1	8
		B.ii.2	9
	B.iii 10–11	B.iii.1	10
		B.iii.2	11
C: 12–13	C.i 12–13	C.i.1	12
		C.i.2	13

With regard to the other chapters from the Book of Micah, De Moor's research is along the same lines presenting abundant evidence for a clear paragraphing of the sections discussed I will not display this material in full. I would like to refer to an interesting detail with regard to Mic. 7:10. Gunkel had argued that the speaking 'I' of Mic. 7:7–10 must have been the female personification of Zion or Jerusalem.[60] A main argument of Gunkel had been the feminine suffix in *'elohāyik* in the bitter question of the enemies to the prophet in 7:10: 'Where is YHWH, your God?'. On the basis of the evidence from the ancient manuscript, De Moor arrived at the view that the speaking voices in Mic. 7:1–6 and 7–10 must have been the same person.[61] Since it is obvious that the speaking voice in 1–6 is a male person the word *'elohāyik* yields a problem. Already in 1963, De Moor had published his discovery that in two Hebrew manuscripts the form *'elohêkā* is attested, with a male suffix.[62] Research in an abundance of Hebrew manuscripts made clear that about 35 % of these manuscripts read the form with a male suffix.[63] This, by implication, weakens the position of Gunkel.

Although De Moor notes that "with regard to paragraphing, the testimony of the ancient manuscripts cannot be accepted uncritically. One must always weigh the total available evidence very carefully",[64] his work is very helpful for the next step in the interpretation of the Book of Micah.

---

60 Gunkel, "Micha-Schluß".
61 De Moor, "Micah 7: 1–13".
62 De Moor, "Handschriften".
63 De Moor, "Micah 7: 1–13", 167.
64 De Moor, "Micah 2: 1–13", 99.

9 Perspectives

Not all problems in the intriguing but enigmatic Book of Micah have been solved by scholars from the low countries. In my view, two important problems remain unsolved:

1. The alternation of the themes of "hope" and "doom" in Micah 2–5;
2. The status of Micah 6–7 in connection with the other chapters.

It seems clear that future research on Micah – in the low countries and elsewhere in the exegetical universe – should be based on the delimitation into smaller units as put forward by the research of the *Pericope*-group.

As for the first problem, I think that a way out of the dilemma could be found by elaborating on the proposal I made a few years ago. Reading Micah 2–5 in the context of Neo-Assyrian prophecies and the so-called Akkadian literary predictive texts, a pattern could be detected.[65] In this pattern of prophetic futurology a distinction is to be made between the immediate future and the times far ahead. History is conceptualized as the interplay of "good times" and "bad times". After the "bad times" of the immediate future prosperous times lay ahead. Phrased differently: the period of 'doom' is only an intermediate phase on the way to real salvation.

As for the second problem, it is clear that Micah 6–7 presents a different voice than Micah 1 and 2–5. Van der Woude's literary-critical division between 1–5 and 6–7 is still valid,[66] but I do not share his conclusion that Deutero-Micah should be depicted as a prophet from Northern Israel living before the fall of Samaria. This date in the eighth century is difficult to substantiate. I would propose to read these chapters as a pseudepigraphic text against a different historical background, namely that of the time of King Josiah. This date can be substantiated with a reference to the conceptual parallels with Assyrian texts from the seventh century.[67] The text joins in the chorus of hope for the restoration of the Davidic dream of unity and for the return of the exiled Samarians.

---

[65] For the Neo-Assyrian prophecies see Nissinen, *Prophets and Prophecy*; the literary predictive texts have been studied by Longman, *Fictional Akkadian Autobiography*; for my proposal see Becking, "Expectations"; "Neo-Assyrian Light".

[66] Van der Woude, "Deutero-Micha".

[67] Compare for instance, the futility clauses in Micah 6:14–15 with a line in the Annals of Sennacherib [Rassam Cylinder IX:65–67; Streck, *Assurbanipal*, 279–85; a curse in the Loyalty Oaths of Esarhaddon [*VTE* = SAA II 6:429–30; see Steymans, *Deuteronomium 28* 101–05]; and the remarks on an early Neo-Babylonian *kudurru* [V. R. 56 = *BBS*, VI ii 51–60].

Much has been done and much more need to be done to unveil the words of a prophetic book that bequeathed the world the moral guidance 'to do justice, and to love kindness, and to walk humbly with your God'?[68]

---

68 Mic. 6:8; ESV; and see the Dutch saying: 'Geen schoner spreuk – en meer van kracht – dan Micha 6 en wel vers 8' [No proverb is more beautiful and powerful than Micah 6 the eighth verse].

Micah in Neo-Assyrian Light

1 Introduction

The Book of Micah is both well-known and complex. Reading through the Hebrew text reveals beautiful poetry full of imaginary language and impressive metaphors. Most readers are familiar with the portrayal of forthcoming peace in Micah 4. The slightly incorrect quotation in the nativity story of Micah 5,1 by Matthew 2,6 has focussed attention on this so-called 'Messianic' prophecy. Micah 6,8 is often seen as foundational for moral piety.[1] The questions on the unity, the coherence and the composition of the Book of Micah, however, bring to light various fissures in the beauty. How to console the harsh words of punishment and doom with the sweat language of salvation? How to consider the difference in tone between Micah 5 and 6–7? These questions have led to an on-going scholarly debate on the emergence and composition of the Book of Micah. This debate has not yet reached a consensus.[2] I therefore feel free to offer my personal view that the book consists of three parts:

- Micah 1   An original, but distorted prophecy
- Micah 2–5 A prophetic futurology based on a variety of reworked sayings from the Micah-tradition
- Micah 6–7 A Josianic treatise based on pseudepigraphy

I will discuss these parts, explain my view on them and explore connections with Neo-Assyrian texts.

2 Micah 1: A Distorted Prophecy

The first chapter of the Book of Micah – in its Masoretic version – seems to be in disorder. Several proposals have been made to reconstruct a more original or fluid text form. Although, I would not like to elaborate wild textual conjectures, the present text in the MT needs some correction in order to be understood. The text itself starts from a description of a theophany moving to a prophecy of doom containing threatening puns on place names. I read this chapter as a prophetic

---

1 See Torrance, "Prophet Micah"; Carroll, "He has told you"; Dreisler, "Micah 6:8".
2 See, e.g., Jeppesen, "New Aspects"; Hillers, *Micah*, 1–9; Vriezen and Van der Woude, *Literature*, 378–80; Kessler, *Micha*, 35–70; Andersen and Freedman, *Micah*, 3–29; Jacobs, "Bridging the Times"; Wöhrle, *Frühen Sammlungen*; Waltke, *Commentary*, 1–16.

https://doi.org/10.1515/9783111208657-006

reflection on the sack of Samaria, that is hinted at the inhabitants of Judah and Jerusalem, especially to those who belief that the divine election have made them invulnerable for inimical threat.

It should be noted that the idea of theophany is a general Ancient Near Eastern pattern.[3] This is true for the religious concept of deities appearing from their divine abode as well as for the literary *genre* describing the effect of this coming in images derived from the world of nature as they are present in Mic. 1,3–4:

> For behold, the LORD is coming forth from His place.
>> He will come down and tread on the high places of the earth.
> The mountains will melt under Him,
>> And the valleys will be split,
> Like wax before the fire,
>> Like water poured down a steep place.

This theme has no parallels in the Neo-Assyrian prophetic text. Note, however, that the phrase 'The mountains will melt under Him' echoes a well-known Ancient near Eastern motif, which can for instance be found in Sumerian hymn in which the theophany of Ninurta is praised:

> Ninurta, before whose roaring the mountains tremble.[4]

Or in a hymn to Marduk:

> By his lightning the steep mountains are destroyed.[5]

Or in a passage in the Ugaritic Baal-cycle:

> His holy voice made the earth,
>> the utterance of his mouth made the mountains tremble.[6]

Micah 1,2 contains an introductory summons that is repeated with variation at Mic. 3,1 and 6,1:

> Hear, O peoples, all of you;
>> Listen, O earth and all it contains

---

3 See Jeremias, *Theophanie*; Scriba, *Theophanie*; Savran "Type Scene".
4 CBS 13936 (STVC 35):58–63; edit. Falkenstein, *Sumerische Götterlieder*, 107–19.
5 K. 3351:16; edit. Ebeling, *Handerhebung*, 94.
6 KTU 1.4 vii:31–32; see Jeremias, *Theophanie*, 87; Dietrich, "Einbau".

This phrase has parallels in various prophetic texts from the Hebrew Bible.[7] A comparable phrase occurs twice in the Neo-Assyrian prophetic texts. On a tablet that collects oracles concerning Babylon and the stabilization of the Royal Assyrian rule a set is oracles from Urkittu-šarrat, a woman from Calah, are preserved.

> The word of Ištar of Arbela, the word of Queen Mulissu:
> I will look
> I will listen
> I will search out the disloyal ones
> And I will put them into the hands of my king
> I will speak to the multitudes:
>> Listen, sun[rise] and sunset[8]!
>> I will create [...][9]

In this oracle of hope for the Assyrian king – this disloyal persons will be delivered in his hands – directs a summon to the whole universe. The contents of the speech, however, are unfortunately broken. In an oracle of salvation we read the following:

> [List]en, o Assyrians!
>> [The king] will vanquish his enemy.
>> [You]r [king] will put his enemy [under] his foot
>> [from] sun[se]t [to] sun[ris]e,
>> [from] sun[ris]e [to] sun[se]t!
>> I will destroy [Meli]d,
>> [I will de]story [...]
>> [I will ....]
>> I will deliver the Cimmerians into his hands
>> and set the land of Ellipi on fire.[10]

The enemy mentioned in this text almost certainly refers to the rebellious brothers of king Esarhaddon. The introductory summons functions as a call for attention for all Assyrians, that Esarhaddon will be victorious – with the help of Aš-šur – both at home and in his forthcoming campaigns.[11]

---

7 See, e.g., Isa. 1,2; 8,9; Amos 3,1.

8 'sun[rise] and sunset' are a clear merism for the earth in its entirety.

9 SAA IX 2 ii:30–37; see Nissinen, *Prophets and Prophecy*, 114–16; note that in the final clause the Assyrian verb *banû*, 'to build; construct' is used for the act of creation; for the concept creation as divine construction see Becking and Korpel, "To Create, to Separate".

10 SAA IX 3 i:27–ii:2. I disagree with Parpola – in his edition – and Nissinen, *Prophets and Prophecy*, 119, by taking the 3d person singular verb-forms (*ik-ta-šad*; *is-sa-kan*) as modal forms – comparable to the Hebrew *perfectum propheticum* – like *a-ḫap-pi*, 'I will destroy'.

11 *Pace* Nissinen, *References*, 100, I do not see here the language of reconciliation.

3 Micah 2–5: Prophetic Futurology

The second part of the Book of Micah, 2–5, is well known for its conceptual and compositional problems. In these chapters an interplay between prophecies of doom and prophecies of salvation can be found as will be explained by the following example. The panorama on peace Micah 4,1–4 is an example of the beauty of Hebrew poetry that is almost impossible to render in a translation:

> In days to come
>> the mountain where the temple stands
> will be the highest one of all,
>> towering above all the hills.
> Many nations will come streaming to it,
>> and their people will say:
> "Let us go up the hill of Yhwh
>> to the temple of Israel's God.
> For He will teach us what He wants us to do;
>> we will walk in the paths he has chosen.
> For Yhwh's teaching comes from Jerusalem;
>> from Zion He speaks to His people".
> He will settle disputes among the nations,
>> among the great powers near and far.
> They will hammer their swords into hoes[12]
>> and their spears into pruning-knives.
> Nations will never again go to war,
>> never prepare for battle again.
> Everyone will live in peace
>> among his own vineyards and fig-trees,
> and no one will make him afraid
>> Yhwh almighty has promised this.

Micah 4 brings us to the core of the conceptual and compositional problems. One problem can be indicated referring to the final words of the previous chapter. Micah 3,12 contains a fierce prophecy of doom:

> Zion will be ploughed like a field,
>> Jerusalem will become a pile of ruins.

Micah 4,1–4 is a vision full of hope with tones of peace and welfare. Micah 3,12 can be seen as an example of the end of time foreshadowing doom and anxiety, here the exile equals the eschaton, while Micah 4,1–4 is written in the language of a consoling perspective of a salvific eschaton. What happened between the two chapters? What is their relation?

---

12 For the translation of *'et*, with 'hoe' and not with the traditional 'ploughshare', see Wagenaar, *Judgment and Salvation*, 138–39.

Here we meet the enigmatic alternation of the themes of 'hope' and 'doom' in Micah. This interchange has been interpreted in different ways. The classical, nineteenth century exegesis and its aftermath have constructed a literary-critical or redaction-historical solution as has been done at various instances in the prophets where the same problem occurs. Wellhausen has depicted the pattern of this redaction in saying that these later redactions offered "Rosen und Lavendel statt Blut und Eisen".[13] In this view Micah is seen as an eighth century prophet of doom – compare Jer. 26 – but during or after the Babylonian exile the traditions on this prophet were enlarged with optimistic phrases borrowed from the school of DtIsa.[14] Some scholars read Micah, or at least Mi. 2–5 as a coherent text.[15] Van der Woude has elaborated an ingenious theory.[16] In his opinion the chapters 2 to 5 of the present Book of Micah contain the text of a dialogue between the pessimistic prophet and some optimistic pseudo-prophets. All views mentioned have strong and weak points. They are not convincing, however. So, I will develop my own view taking into account the position of Hillers[17] who characterizes Micah as 'millenarian', or a prophet of a New Age. In Hillers' view Micah foresees the coming of times of trouble before the onset of a golden Messianic age.[18]

As is well known, there are striking similarities between this text in Micah 4 and Isaiah 2. The scholarly discussion on this point did not reach a consensus yet.[19] Van der Woude elaborated the view, that the optimistic opponents of Micah

---

13 Wellhausen, *Kleine Propheten*, 96.

14 Wellhausen, *Kleine Propheten*, 142–143. See also, e.g., Jeremias, "Deutung"; Mays, *Micah*; Collins, *Mantle*, 72–73; Nogalski, *Literary Precursors*, 123–70; McKane, *Micah*, 17–19; Kessler, *Micha*, 41–47; Wagenaar, *Judgment and Salvation*.

15 E.g., Hagstrom, *Coherence*; Utzschneider, *Michas Reise*, 152–164; Dempsey, "Micah 2–3", 117–28; Wood, "Speech and Action", 645–62; Jacobs, *Conceptual Coherence*; Runions, *Changing Subjects*, 133–65; Bail, *Verzogene Sehnsucht*, 75–142; Smith-Christopher, "Refashioned Weapons"; Waltke, *Micah*, 143–342.

16 Van der Woude, "Micah in Dispute"; Van der Woude, *Micha*, esp. 61–192; see also Vriezen and Van der Woude, *Literature*, 382–84; Boogaart, *Reflections on Restoration*, 49–88; Strydom, *Micah*, 127–57.

17 Hillers, *Micah*, 4–8.

18 Hillers, *Micah*, 6.

19 The four possibilities –
a. Micah is original, it was borrowed by Isaiah;
b. Isaiah is original, it was borrowed by Micah (or the editors of this book);
c. both have adopted an already existing hymn from the Jerusalem cult-tradition;
d. the text is a late interpolation in both books
are all defended in the various commentaries and studies on Micah with a preference for the final one. McKane, *Micah*, 117–27, argues that the unit is a post-exilic insertion both in Micah and Isaiah; Kessler, *Micha*, 178–81, opts for the emergence of the textual unit from the Micaian tradition; Sweeney, "Micah's Debate", construes the two texts to represent different voices in a

are quoting here Isaiah as an objection against Micah's prophecy of doom. Their argument would have been: You might prophesy doom and exile; the great prophet Isaiah, however, already said something else.[20] Van der Woude's view is attractive to some degree especially since he is pointing to a very early example of abusing Scripture by quoting it. But is he right? I will try to show that a meaningful interpreting is possible accepting that Micah himself is quoting here Isaiah. The answer to two questions will lead to this possible interpretation.

1) What is the meaning of the expression 'in the end of the days'?
2) Which character does the prophecy of salvation eventually has?

1) The Hebrew phrase *bᵉʾaḥrît hayyāmmîm* can be compared with the Akkadian idiom *ina aḥrat umî*. Both refer to a point in time. In the near future a turn in the sense of a decisive change will take place. *bᵉʾaḥrît hayyāmmîm* refers to a decisive turn in time, but not the end of time, rather the end of a period and the beginning of a new one.[21] The salvation described in Micah 4 is hoped to take place in the future, but within the limits of time and Israelite history after the people went through a period of chastening.

2) The contents of hope.[22] In abstract: the world to come viewed by Micah is the reversal of the world he is now living in. Dark and light, black and white are interchanged. This image from the world of photography might be a metaphor for Micah's message.[23]

– In the *yet* of Micah Jerusalem and Zion are peripheral in the Assyrian empire. Jerusalem is the tiny capital city of a kingdom with not much rule in the international politics of the days. It is just another state in the area of Syria and Palestine. But *then* it will be the center of the world.
– *Yet* the people are coming to Jerusalem for battle and conquest. *Then* they will come to Jerusalem to learn the way of God. 'Path' and 'way' are metaphors for how to behave, for attitude and conduct.[24]

---

debate on how to cope with the Persian imperial power; Rudman, "Zechariah 8:20–22", tends to the view that the Book of Micah has transmitted the original form of the oracle. Hillers, *Micha*, 53, states that "it would be fatuous to suppose that one could at this date settle the question of the authorship of Micah 4:1–5".
20 Van der Woude, "Micah in Dispute"; Van der Woude, "Micah IV 1–5"; Van der Woude, *Micha*, 125–32.
21 E.g. Kosmala, "At the End"; Hillers, *Micah*, 50; Utzschneider, *Michas Reise*, 152; Wagenaar, *Judgment and Salvation*, 28–31; Jacobs, *Conceptual Coherence*, 145.
22 On the concept of hope in the Hebrew Bible see: Zimmerli, *Man and his Hope*; Knierim, *Task*, 244–68. I disagree with Smith-Christopher, "Refashioned Weapons", who considers the language in Mic. 4,1–3 to be hyperbolic and not the expression of a utopia people could long for.
23 See also the remarks by Brueggemann, *Theology*, 499–502.593–95.
24 See Zehnder, *Wegmetaphorik*.

- *Yet* they are having swords and spears. They are symbols of warfare indicating that scarce natural resources of iron are abused for war. *Then* they will be transformed into hoes and pruning-knives. These are symbols of agricultural life in which they serve mankind in his struggle for food.
- *Yet* people are solving their problems by warfare. *Then* they will solve their problems by following the impetus of the *thôrah* from YHWH.[25]
- *Yet* the acres are laying waste. The harvest is broken or stolen by soldiers. *Then* everyone will live in peace among his own vineyards and fig trees, and no one will make him afraid. This formula is used as a description of abundance and undisturbed peace and security. Vineyard and fig tree are well-known symbols describing the abundance of the Holy Land. The Egyptian novelist Sinuhe called the land 'Iaa':

> It was a fair land, called Iaa
> There were figs there and grapes.
> It had wine more abundant than water
> Its honey was plentiful, its plant-oil innumerable
> On its trees were all kinds of fruit
> There was barley there and wheat,
> And unlimited cattle of every kind.[26]

In Micah 4 these transformations are phrased in a literary pattern. This pattern is called: concentric symmetry. When such a from is the expression of reversal or transformation, than the most central textual element contains the motor which stimulates the changes. In the middle of the Micaian oracle the phrases stand:

> For YHWH's teaching comes from Jerusalem;
> from Zion He speaks to His people.

The forthcoming changes are effected by a change in God. He will turn himself towards mankind in spite of the sinful behavior described in Ch. 2 and 3.

Although Van der Woude has given an interesting interpretation, I will offer a differing view: The prophet Micah had to bring a message of doom. This was necessary within the framework of his time: the people of Israel had offended the relationship with God, by transgressing the religious and social code implied in that relationship. At the same time Micah knows about God's love and divine salvation. Both – doom and salvation – are brought together in a two level prophetic message. The first level is the prophecy of immediate doom as punishment. Doom, however, is not God's final word. In a more distant future Israel will be

---

25 See Albertz, "Konfliktschlichtung".
26 Sinuhe: 81–84. The land 'Iaa' probably refers to the district of Araru in Retenu (Canaan).

created anew within the dimensions of God's salvation. In order to describe this second level, Micah has borrowed the imagery of his great predecessor Isaiah.

In the meantime a pattern has been developed that is characteristic for the prophetic futurology. This pattern might be called: the chastening pattern. Threat, conquest, downfall, exile etc. are interpreted as divine acts in history. They are, however, not the end of time or history. Through the humiliation a new future is possible. This future can be reached by conversion[27] or by new deeds of the deity, as is the proclamation of Deutero-Isaiah.

Before coming to my conclusions, I would like to pay attention to another prophetic text from the Hebrew Bible: Jer. 30–31, the so-called little book of consolation. In my opinion the material in Jer. 30–31 is authentic from the prophet. This means that I am not convinced by the arguments for a literary-critical[28] or redaction-historical[29] view on the emergence of these two chapters.[30] Jer. 30–31 reflects the fall of Jerusalem in 587 BCE. The words in it were spoken after the ruination of temple and city. In the second part of the Book of Consolation three times the phrase; 'Behold, the days are coming – oracle of the LORD' occurs (Jer. 31,27.31.38). This phrase, like b^e*aḥrît hayyāmmîm* in Micah 4, refers to a future not too far away. The general pattern in these chapters is, that now the city of Jerusalem is fallen and Judah has gone into exile, YHWH will turn his face towards Israel and give the people a new future. The threefold repetition contains three elements:

1)   now the LORD will plant them and build them up;
2)   the new covenant;
3)   the rebuilding of the city.

So the well-known text on the new covenant in their hearts is part of a wider context, which prohibits an all too quick Christological interpretation. After the process of chastening – the Babylonian exile is interpreted as such – history will go on and there will be a new relationship between God and his people. One characteristic of the new relationship is the new covenant in which everyone is personally responsible for his deeds and attitude. The saying "the parents ate the sour grapes, but the children got the sour taste" is no longer of value. This new covenant will be put and written in the hearts of the people. 'Heart' here is a metaphor for the decisive orientation in life.[31]

---

27 As is the theology of the Book of Kings; see, e.g., Nelson, *Historical Books*, 129–48; Römer, *Deuteronomistic History*.
28 Mowinckel, *Komposition*.
29 Schmid, *Buchgestalten*.
30 Becking, *Fear and Freedom*.
31 Becking, *Fear and Freedom*, 244–72.

Both in Micah and in Jeremiah a pattern can be detected.[32] In this prophetic view, history is a display of an interchange between 'good times' and 'bad times'. All texts imply the idea that there is an alternation in time from periods of prosperity to times of trouble and from situations of sorrow to a period of peace. Fear and freedom follow each other in an on-going interplay. This worldview can be characterised as proto-apocalyptic. In later apocalyptic literature history is related in a schematic way. The past is presented in periods. I will characterise this prophetic view as *proto*-apocalyptic since the concept of periodizing in its extreme form is not yet present. Besides, the active role of the divine being is stressed. I would add that a comparable worldview is attested in Mesopotamian texts that are roughly contemporaneous with 'Micah'. In the so-called Accadian literary predictive texts the same pattern of interchange between 'good times' and 'bad times' is detectable.[33]

A very interesting text in this connection is "text A".[34] In this text history and future are periodized into the reigns of a great number of kings and princes who will rule. The rule of a bad prince is indicated as follows:

> The sanctuaries of the great gods will be confused.
> The defeat of Akkad will be decreed.
> There will be confusion, disorder and unfortunate events in the land.
> The great will be made small.[35]

The reign of a good king is depicted in the reverse image:

> He will re-establish the regular offering for the Igigi-gods which was cut off.
> Favourable winds will blow
> Abundance in the midst of [...]
> Cattle [will lie down] safely in the steppe[36]

The text in its present though broken form ends with the depiction of a bad prince in whose reign:

> [The one who was rich] will stretch out his hand to the poor
> [...] the mother will speak what is right to her daughter.
> [...] advice to the land, advice [...] consume the land
> The king will bring hard times on the land.[37]

---

32 See also texts like Amos 6,12; Jer. 2,32; 8,4; 18,14.
33 De Jong Ellis, "Observations"; Longman, *Akkadian Autobiography*; Neujahr, "Royal Ideology".
34 KAR 421; Grayson and Lambert, "Akkadian Prophecies"; Longman, *Akkadian Autobiography*, 512-63.240-42.
35 KAR 421 ii:11'–14'; Longman, *Akkadian Autobiography*, 241.
36 KAR 421 iii:1'–8'; Longman, *Akkadian Autobiography*, 241.
37 KAR 421 rev. ii:10'–18'; Longman, *Akkadian Autobiography*, 242.

In the fictional autobiography of the god Marduk the disastrous situation in Babylon after the deity had to abandon his country, is described in graphic language. I will mention a few of the images:

> Aristocrats stretch out their hands (to beg) to the commoner
>
> ...
>
> Dogs go mad and bite people.
> As many as they bite do not live, they die.[38]

After he had fulfilled his days the deity carried himself back to Babylon, where circumstances turned for the better.

The theme of reversal is not only present in the Accadian literary predictive texts, but also elsewhere in the Ancient Near East. The hymn that was composed on the occasion of the coronation of the neo-Assyrian king Ashurbanipal is full of language and metaphors that express the traditional Mesopotamian view on the just king.[39] After the singing of this hymn, the king had to pronounce a blessing before Shamash – a blessing that recollects the themes from the loyalty oaths that Esarhaddon had concluded with his vassals shortly before his death and thus not long before Ashurbanipal's inauguration –. One of the lines read:

> He who speaks with the king or treasonably,
> if he is a notable, he will die a violent death,
> if he is a rich man, he will become poor.[40]

In the Egyptian admonitions of Ipuwer – from the first intermediate period – the imagery language of a world turned topsy-turvy functions as an indication for a 'bad time':

> Behold, he who slept wifeless through want [finds] riches,
>   while he whom he never saw stands making dole.
> Behold, he who had no property
>   is now a possessor of wealth, and the magnate praises him.
> Behold, the poor of the land have become rich,
>   and the [erstwhile owner] of property is one who has nothing.
> Behold, serving-men have become masters of butlers,
>   and he who was once a messenger now sends someone else.
> Behold, he who had no loaf is now the owner of a barn,
>   and his storehouse is provided with the goods of another.
> Behold, he whose hair is fallen out and who had no oil
>   has now become the possessors of jars of sweet myrrh.

---

38 Borger, "Gott Marduk", 8.16; Longman, *Akkadian Autobiography*, 234.
39 Arneth, "Šamaš".
40 SAA III 11:rev.9–10.

> Behold, she who had no box is now the owner of a coffer,
> and she who had to look at her face in the water is now the owner of a mirror.[41]

In this connection, attention should be paid to the well-known Cyrus-cylinder. This inscription is often seen as extra-biblical evidence for the historicity of the decree of Cyrus in Ezra 1. The inscription has been interpreted as showing a liberal policy of respect toward other religions. The inscription would show that Cyrus' policy toward the descendants of the Judaean exiles was not unique but fitted the pattern of his rule. Amelia Kuhrt, however, has made clear that the inscription is of a propagandistic and stereotypical nature.[42] The return of divine images and people related in Cyrus Cylinder 30–34, if not mere propaganda, refers to measures taken on a local scale. It concerns divine images from cities surrounding Babylon, brought back to the shrines from where they were exiled by Nabonidus.[43] This passage has nothing to do with Judaeans, Jews or Jerusalem.[44] The text is a reflection of the worldview of the Marduk priests of the Esaǧila temple at Babylon. They casted Cyrus in the role of a 'good prince' who replaced the 'bad prince' Nabonidus. In their view the rise to power of Cyrus was an indication of the beginning of a new and good era as could be seen in the return of the divine images. Cyrus is seen as acting with divine blessing:

> Marduk surveyed and looked throughout the lands, searching for a righteous king, his favourite. He called out his name: Cyrus, king of Anšan; he pronounced his name to be king all over the world. He made the land of Gutium and all the Umman-manda [i.e., the Medes] bow in submission at his feet. And he [i.e., Cyrus] shepherded with justice and righteousness all the black-headed people, over whom he [i.e., Marduk] had given him victory. Marduk, the great lord, guardian of his people, looked with gladness upon his good deeds and upright heart.[45]

His predecessor, the Babylonian king Nabonidus is shaped as a villain. In contrast, Cyrus' acts are glorious and righteous:

> When I entered Babylon in a peaceful manner, I took up my lordly abode in the royal palace amidst rejoicing and happiness. Marduk, the great lord, established as his fate for me a magnanimous heart of one who loves Babylon, and I daily attended to his worship. My vast army marched into Babylon in peace; I did not permit anyone to frighten the people of Sumer and Akkad. I sought the welfare of the city of Babylon and all its sacred centres. As for the citizens of Babylon, [...] upon whom Nabonidus imposed a corvée which

---

41 Ipuwer 8,1–5; *COS* I, 96; Enmarch, *Ipuwer.*
42 Kuhrt, "Cyrus Cylinder".
43 Kuhrt, "Cyrus Cylinder".
44 Kuhrt, "Cyrus Cylinder", 87–88.
45 Cyrus Cylinder: 11–14.

was not the gods' wish and not befitting them, I relieved their wariness and freed them from their service. Marduk, the great lord, rejoiced over my good deeds. He sent gracious blessing upon me, Cyrus, the king who worships him, and upon Cambyses, the son who is my offspring, and upon all my army, and in peace, before him, we moved around in friendship.[46]

By reading Micah 2–5 within this conceptual framework, a significant reading of the textual unit is evoked. To the author of the Book of Micah, the exile does not equal the eschaton. The forthcoming exiliation of the inhabitants of Judah and the ruination of the city of Jerusalem – both took place some 125 years after the prophet Micah is generally assumed to have uttered his words – is not the end of history and certainly not seen as the end of the divine exertion and sustenance. This implies that a message can be read from the Book of Micah that is consoling for the *personae miserae* of all places and in all times.[47]

This section of the Book of Micah is therefore not specifically influenced by Neo-Assyrian texts, or prophecies. My analysis of the temporal aspects and the interpretation of the interplay between prophecies of doom and prophecies of salvation, make clear that its author(s) shared the common theology of the Ancient Near East. This way of world-making with regard to the near and distant future[48] shows that Micah 2–5 was, despite its specific Yahwistic position, a child of his time.

Before moving to the final section in the Book of Micah, I would like to refer to an interesting parallel with a neo-Assyrian text. Mic. 3,6 contains the following prophecy of doom:

> Therefore *it will be* night for you – without vision,
> And darkness for you – without divination.[49]

The theme of prophetic silence functions as underpinning the very bitterness of Judah's fate. In days to come Yhwh will leave his people and the traditional channels for communication – divination and prophecy – will be closed. In the coming darkness Yhwh will be out of reach, the people of Judah are left on its own. The theme is also present in a lengthy letter written by Urad-Gula to the king. Urad-Gula[50] had been an exorcist in the service of Esarhaddon and Assur-

---

46 Cyrus Cylinder: 22–28.

47 Kessler, *Micha*, 53–70.

48 Goodman, *Ways of Worldmaking*, 1–22.

49 See, e.g., Van der Woude, *Micha*, 106–117; Hillers, *Micah*, 44–46; Dempsey, "Micah 2–3", 125; Kessler, *Micha*, 151–59; Wood, "Speech and Action", 657–58; Andersen and Freedman, *Micah*, 357–77; De Jong, *Isaiah*, 326; Waltke, *Micah*, 157–75.

50 Parpola, "Forlorn Scholar"; Van der Toorn, "Lion's Den", Van der Toorn, *Scribal Culture*, 61–62.

banipal. He was a member of a prominent Assyrian scribal family, he was the son of Esarhaddon's chief exorcist Adad-šumu-uṣur[51] and the nephew of Esarhaddon's master scholar Nabu-zeru-lešir. The fate in the life of Urad-Gula had turned, he is impoverished, he lost his position, his wife is severely ill. He felt his life was as in the lion's den.[52] He turns to the king for help is his old age in a complaint drenched in melancholic language. Part of his complaint is

> [The king] is not pleased with me; I go to the palace, I am no good; [I turned to] a prophet (but) did not find [any hop]e, he was adverse and did not see much. [O king] my [lord], seeing you is happiness, your attention is fortune.[53]

The absence of a vision at a prophet deprives him of his last hope.

4 Micah 6–7

In the final chapters of the Book of Micah a different voice can be heard. Van der Woude's literary-critical division between 1–5 and 6–7 is still valid,[54] but I do not share his conclusion that Deutero-Micah should be depicted as a prophet from Northern Israel living before the fall of Samaria. I propose to read this pseudepigraphic text against a different historical horizon, namely that of the times of King Josiah. Then the text shares the choir of hope for restoration of the Davidic dream of unity and for return of the exiled Samarians. An interesting question would be, why these chapters were added to the book of Micah? As yet, I don't have an answer to that question.

In Mic. 6–7 no parallels with the Neo-Assyrian prophecies can be found. The two chapters, however, contain a few references to the language of the Neo-Assyrian vassal-treaties and loyalty oath especially to the futility-clauses.[55] This observation underscores a date in the Josianic age, which was a period in which Judah was liberating itself from the burden of being a vassal of Assyria. The oracle in Mic. 6,9–16 ends with a set of predictions that resemble the futility-clauses in the curses in the Neo-Assyrian texts just mentioned:

---

51 See on him: Deller, "Adad-šumu-Usur".
52 Van der Toorn, "Lion's Den".
53 SAA X 294: r.30–33; see on this letter Nissinen, *References to Prophecy*, 84–88; Nissinen, *Prophets and Prophecy*, 158–63; with Nissinen, *Prophets and Prophecy*, 162, I am not convinced by reading: *la-a a-mur-ma aḫ-ḫur ù di-ig-lu*, to be translated: 'I did not see [happiness] thereafter and my eyesight is diminishing', as proposed by De Jong, *Isaiah*, 292–93.
54 Van der Woude, "Deutero-Micha", 365–78.
55 Hillers, *Treaty-Curses*, 28–29; Hillers, *Micah*, 80–82.

You will eat,
>   but you will not be satisfied,
And your vileness will be in your midst.
You will *try to* remove *for safekeeping,*
>   But you will not preserve *anything,*
And what you do preserve
>   I will give to the sword.
You will sow but
>   you will not reap.
You will tread the olive but
>   will not anoint yourself with oil;
And the grapes,
>   but you will not drink wine. (Mic. 6,14–15)

The language of the futility clause has deep roots in the Ancient Near East. In a *kudurru* of the twelfth century BCE Babylonian king Nebuchadnezzar I, one can read that a trespasser will be severely punished:

> In the anger of their heart may the great gods plan evil against him, so that, another may own the house he built. With a dagger in his neck and a poniard in his eyes, may he cast down his face before his captor and may the latter, unmindful of his pleading, quickly cut off his life. In the collapse of his house may his hands get into the mire, as long as he lives may he drag along misery, and as long as heaven and earth exist may his seed perish.[56]

The phrase 'The house that he has built, someone else will take it into possession' is a clear example of a futility clause. The theme is adapted in a curse in the Loyalty Oaths of Esarhaddon:

> May your sons not take possession of your house
>   But a strange enemy will divide your goods.[57]

A comparable futility clause is present in the report in the annals of Assurbanipal on his war against Arab tribes:

> The camels' calves, the young donkeys, calves, and lambs will suckle up to seven times with nourishing (animals), but they will not satiate their bellies with milk.[58]

The same imagery, but not phrased as futility-clauses, is already present in the Sumerian Lamentation on the destruction of Ur(im):

---

56 V R. 56 = *BBS*, VI ii 51–60; see also Steymans, *Deuteronomium 28*, 123.
57 *VTE* = SAA II 6:429–30; see also Steymans, *Deuteronomium 28*, 101–05.
58 Rassam Cylinder IX:65–67; Streck, *Assurbanipal*, 279–85.

My city no longer multiplies for me like good ewes,
    its good shepherd is gone.
Urim no longer multiplies for me like good ewes,
    its shepherd boy is gone.
My bull no longer crouches in its cow-pen,
    its herdsman is gone.
My sheep no longer crouch in their fold,
    their herdsman is gone.
In the river of my city dust has gathered,
    and the holes of foxes have been dug there.
In its midst no flowing water is carried,
    its tax-collector is gone.
In the fields of my city there is no grain,
    their farmer is gone.
My fields, have grown tangled (?) weeds,
    like fields from which the hoe has been kept away (?).
My orchards and gardens that produced abundant syrup and wine
    have grown mountain thornbushes.
My plain that used to be covered in its luxurious verdure
    has become cracked (?) like a kiln.[59]

The following unit is the woe-oracle, Mic. 7,1–7.[60] This unit elaborates the curse(s) in 6,14–15 by moulding them into the language of change. In doing so, the picture of a devastated and chaotic country is evoked. Despair and confusion are presented in the language of a world topsy turvy. I will give two examples:

The best of them is like a briar,
    The most upright like a thorn hedge. (Mic. 7,4)

For son treats father contemptuously,
    Daughter rises up against her mother (Mic. 7,6)

It should be noted that although no exact parallels can be found, the pattern of change as present in the Accadian literary predictive texts discussed above, is clearly detectable. No parallels to the curses in the Neo-Assyrian treaties and loyalty oaths can be found.

The final section of the Book of Micah, 7,8–20, offers a reversal of the reversed imaginary. It is the compassion of God that will open a lane for new life. The language used in this unit has no parallels to Neo-Assyrian texts with one minor exception. In a prophecy of doom for the nations their fate is depicted – among other images – as follows:

---

59 *The lament for Urim (http://etcsl.orinst.ox.ac.uk text 2.2.2):265–274; see also Wood, "Speech and Action".*
60 On this literary Form see, e.g., Janzen, *Mourning Cry*; Hillers, *"Hôy* and the *Hôy-*Oracles".

> They will lick the dust like a serpent,
>> like reptiles of the earth. (Mic. 7,17)

This line reminds one of a curse in treaty between the Assyrian king Aššur-nerari and Mati'-ilu, the king of Arpad:

> May Adad, the canal inspector of heaven and earth,
> Put an end to Mati'-ilu's land
> And the people of his land through hunger, want, and famine
>
> ...
>
> may dust be their food
>
> ...
>
> And may their sleeping place be in the dung heap.[61]

5 Micah in Neo-Assyrian Light

What conclusions can be drawn? It should be noted that no clear influence from the Neo-Assyrian prophecies or the curses in the vassal treaties and loyalty-oaths could be detected. The few parallels that were found, are of a more general character. The expression אל־תירא, 'do not fear', is absent in the Book of Micah. What can be observed is an adaptation of general themes like theophany and the interplay on 'good times / bad times'. It is only a shallow light that shines on Micah. In this regard the book differs from later prophetic literature, such as Isaiah,[62] Nahum, Jeremiah and DtIsaiah. This factum might be an indication for two features: (1) Greater parts of the Book of Micah were written before the cultural influence of Assyria was settled in Judah and Israel. (2) Micah – and its tradents – were situated in a position in society that was less influenced by Assyrian culture.

---

61 SAA III 2 iv:8–12.
62 Isa. 1–39 in its various redactions, see De Jong, *Isaiah*.

Religious Polemics in the Book of Micah

1 Divine Incomparability assumes Monolatry

The doxology at the end of the Book of Micah[1] contains a praise of the incomparability[2] of Yнwн:

> Who is a God like Thee, who pardons iniquity
>> and passes over the rebellious act of the remnant of His possession?
> He does not retain His anger forever,
>> Because He delights in unchanging love.[3]

A few remarks need to be made. The doxology at the end of the book was most probably added by the final redactor of the Book of Micah. This view is, of course, in need of an argument. It is, however, not the aim of this contribution to sketch the redactional and compositional history of the Book of Micah or to discuss the question whether or not the redactional process concurred with the emergence of the 'Book of the Twelve'.[4] Suffice it to make two observations. (1) Micah 7,18 contains a pun of the name of the prophet – as has often been remarked –. The words *mî 'ēl kāmôkā*, 'who is a god like you', resemble the name of the prophet: *mîkā*, which as such is a shortening of a theophoric name *mîkā'ēl/mîkāyā*, 'who is like God/Yнwн'.[5] (2) Micah 7,18–20 contains all sorts of theological evaluations of Israel's history with God that are written in a register of language different from the rest of the Book of Micah.

---

1 Mic. 7,18–20.
2 On this concept see Labuschagne, *Incomparability*; Brettler, *Metaphorical Mapping*; Clifford, "Deutero-Isaiah"; Olson, "God for Us".
3 Mic. 7,18; see, e.g., Van der Woude, *Micha*, 263–67; Wolff, *Micha*, 204–08; Hillers, *Micah*, 87–91; Brueggemann, *Theology*, 141–42; Peacock, "Who is a God"; Roth, *Israel und die Völker*, 182–205; Jeremias, *Propheten*, 222–225; Decorzant, *Gericht*.
4 See, e.g., Nogalski, *Literary Precursors*, 123–70; Collins, *Mantle*; Jones, *Formation*; Redditt and Schart (eds), *Thematic Threads*; Wöhrle, *Frühen Sammlungen*; Wöhrle, *Abschluss des Zwölfprophetenbuches*; Albertz, Nogalski and Wöhrle (eds), *Perspectives*.
5 See Albertz and Schmitt, *Family and Household Religion*, 575.

Note: It is with great pleasure that I dedicate this essay to Hans Barstad. Out of our discussion over a pizza in Louvain 1989 grew friendship and an exchange of ideas. Hans's communications – both written and orally – always urged me to rethink my position(s) and to improve the methodological fabric of my argument.

https://doi.org/10.1515/9783111208657-007

In this doxology, the incomparability of YHWH is not only given testimony of, the statement is argued with references to his character: YHWH is a God of exemplary forgiveness.[6] This attribute makes him different from other deities. It should be noted that proclaiming YHWH's incomparability assumes (1) the acceptance of the existence of other deities and (2) a denunciation of these deities and their veneration.[7]

Almost fifty years ago – that is before the discussions on the Jahweh-Allein Bewegung[8] and before the find of the inscriptions referring to 'Yahweh and his Asherah' – Labuschagne made an important remark: 'The fact that Israel *did as a matter of fact compare its God with other gods* confirms that they took the existence of other gods seriously'.[9] This observation brings him to the conclusion that the religion in Ancient Israel cannot be construed as expressing intolerant or absolute monotheism.[10] This view is nowadays – after the great discussion on monotheism in the 1990-ties – almost generally accepted. In my view the incomparability of YHWH implies a form of monolatry: It was only YHWH who should be venerated by the Israelites the main 'argument' being his loving kindness and trustworthy guidance of the people.[11] The question is, however, what kind of monolatry is involved. Does the doxology at the end of the Book of Micah imply the veneration of a variety of divine beings in Ancient Israel? Or is something like Mono-Yahwism at stake?[12] This would imply that the doxology is promoting a specific form of Yahwism detrimental to other forms of Yahwism.

2 Other Gods

Different from the Book of Amos,[13] no other divine beings are mentioned by name in the Book of Micah. The only instance where other gods are referred to is Micah 4,5. The vision on what will happen in days to come, is concluded in Micah as follows:

---

6 See Brueggemann, *Theology*, 117–313; Newman, "Balancing".
7 See Labuschagne, *Incomparability*; Kessler, *Micha*, 309.
8 As labelled by Lang, *Einzige Gott*; see also Lang, "Jahwe-allein-Bewegung".
9 Labuschagne, *Incomparability*, 144
10 Labuschagne, *Incomparability*, 142–49.
11 See among many other publications: Penchansky, *Twilight*; Heiser, "Monotheism"; Olyan, "Isaiah 40–55".
12 On the concept of Mono-Yahwism see Lang, *Einzige Gott*, and recently, Hutton, "Local Manifestations"; Becking, "Ambivalence".
13 See Barstad, *Religious Polemics*.

Although all people walk
    each in the name of his god,
as for us, we have to walk
    in the name of Y<small>HWH</small>, our God forever and ever.[14]

As is well known, there are striking similarities between the text in Micah 4,1–4 and Isaiah 2. The scholarly discussion on this point has not yet reached a consensus.[15] Van der Woude elaborated the view that the optimistic opponents of Micah are quoting here Isaiah as an objection against Micah's prophecy of doom. Their argument would have been: 'You might prophesy doom and exile; the great prophet Isaiah, however, has already said something else'.[16] Van der Woude's view is attractive to some degree, especially since he is pointing to a very early example of abusing Scripture by quoting it. But is he right? I shall try to show that a meaningful interpretation is possible accepting that Micah himself is quoting Isaiah here. The answers to two questions will lead to this possible interpretation.

(1) What is the meaning of the expression "in the end of the days"?
(2) Which character does the prophecy of salvation eventually has?

(1) The Hebrew phrase b^e'aḥrît hayyāmîm can be compared with the Akkadian idiom ina aḥrat umî. Both refer to a point in time. In the near future a turn, in the sense of a decisive change, will take place. b^e'aḥrît hayyāmîm refers to a decisive turn in time, but not the end of time; rather, the end of a period and the

---

14 Mic. 4,5; *pace* Barstad, *Religious Polemics*, 186, I do not think that this verse stands isolated in its context, since the lines draw a conclusion with regard of the moral conduct of Judah; see also the poetic arguments in Andersen, Freedman, *Micah*, 425–27; and Brueggemann, *Theology*, 171; Jensen, "Micah 4: 1–5"; Bail, *Verzogene Sehnsucht*, 117–22; Jeremias, *Propheten*, 168–77.

15 The four possibilities are:

a. Micah is original and was borrowed by Isaiah;

b. Isaiah is original and was borrowed by Micah (or the editors of this book);

c. both have adopted an already existing hymn from the Jerusalem cult-tradition;

d. the text is a late interpolation in both books.

These are all defended in the various commentaries and studies on Micah, with a majority preference for the final one; see also the outline in Andersen, Freedman, *Micah*, 415–25. McKane, *Micah*, 117–27, argues that the unit is a post-exilic insertion in both Micah and Isaiah; Kessler, *Micha*, 178–81; Wagenaar, *Judgment and Salvation*, 261–73, opt for the emergence of the textual unit from the Micah tradition; Sweeney, "Micah's Debate", construes the two texts to represent different voices in a debate on how to cope with the Persian imperial power; Rudman, "Zechariah 8:20–22", tends to the view that the Book of Micah has transmitted the original form of the oracle. Hillers, *Micah*, 53, states that "it would be fatuous to suppose that one could at this date settle the question of the authorship of Micah 4:1–5."

16 Van der Woude, "Micah in Dispute"; Van der Woude, "Micah IV 1–5"; Van der Woude, *Micha*, 125–32.

beginning of a new one.[17] The salvation described in Micah 4 is expected to take place in the future, but within the limits of time and Israelite history after the people have gone through a period of chastening.

(2) The content of the hope[18] may be summarized thus: the world to come viewed by Micah is the reverse of the world he is now living in. Dark and light, black and white are interchanged. This image from the world of photography might be a metaphor for Micah's message.[19]

All this implies, that I construe Mic. 4,1–4 to be part of the original layer of the Book of Micah. The text expresses a future that will come after the period of doom that is described in various sections of Micah 2–5.[20] The conclusion in verse 5 needs to be read in the context reversal imaginary of Micah 4,1–4. In the light of the forthcoming reversal of the world-order, Israel is summoned to take Yhwh as their moral compass during the interim period of decline, desperation and destruction that is seen by Micah for the imminent future.

The summons expresses an aspect of common ancient Near Eastern theology.[21] According to a wider understanding, the god(s) had each their own territory.[22] This common precursor of the idea *cuius regio, eius religio*[23] is, however, given a specific twist in the context of Micah 4. The forthcoming doom might have yielded the idea of the powerlessness or incapacity of Yhwh. Despite the disaster, Israel is summoned to remain faithful in the expectation of reversal of fates.

The 'gods of the nations' are unnamed here. This implies that no specific deities are mentioned. Yet, the mentioning underscores the fact that by Micah their existence was taken seriously.[24]

3 Customs, Acts and Morality

Religion, however, is more than only knowing the name of the divine being. Any religion is a system that contains a set of beliefs, cultural values, a world-view,

---

17 E.g. Kosmala, "End of the Days"; Hillers, *Micah*, 50; Utzschneider, *Michas Reise*, 152; Andersen, Freedman, *Micah*, 401–02; Wagenaar, *Judgment and Salvation*, 28–31; Jacobs, *Conceptual Coherence*, 145.
18 On the concept of hope in the Hebrew Bible see Zimmerli, *Man and his Hope*; Knierim, *Task*, 244–68. I disagree with Smith-Christopher, "Refashioned Weapons", who considers the language in Mic. 4,1–3 to be hyperbolic and not the expression of a utopia for which people could long.
19 See also the remarks by Brueggemann, *Theology*, 499–502.593–95.
20 See also Becking, "Expectations".
21 See Smith, "Common Theology".
22 See, e.g., Block, *Gods*.
23 See Zimmermann, *Augsburger Religionsfrieden*.
24 See also Kessler, *Micha*, 187–88, 309

moral values that expresses itself in a variety of rituals quite often based on shared mythology.[25] I will not enter here in a broad discussion a various types of definition of the concept of 'religion', but apply some sort of functional idea of the concept to the texts in the Book of Micah by putting the question: Does the Book contain traces of dispute on the function of Yahwism in Ancient Israel?

Before answering that question in detail, I would like to have a look at the Book of Micah in general. The Book of Micah is both well-known and complex. Reading through the Hebrew text reveals beautiful poetry full of imaginary and impressive metaphors. Most readers are familiar with the portrayal of end-time peace in Mic. 4,1–4 just referred to. The slightly incorrect quotation of Mic. 5,1 by Matt. 2,6, in the Nativity account, has focussed attention on this so-called "Messianic" prophecy. Mic. 6:8 is often seen as foundational for moral piety.[26] Questions about the unity, the coherence, and the composition of the Book of Micah, however, bring to light various fissures in the beauty. How may we reconcile the harsh words of punishment and doom with the sweet language of salvation? How may we explain the difference in tone between Micah 5 and 6–7? These questions have led to an on-going scholarly debate on the emergence and composition of the Book of Micah. This debate has not yet reached a consensus.[27] I therefore feel free to offer my personal view that the book consists of three parts:

- Micah 1   An original, but distorted prophecy
- Micah 2–5   A prophetic futurology based on a variety of reworked sayings from the Micah tradition
- Micah 6–7   A Josianic treatise based on pseudepigraphy

3.1 Transgressing the Moral Code (Micah 1)

The first chapter of the Book of Micah – in its Masoretic version – seems to be in disorder. Several proposals have been made to reconstruct a more original or fluid text form. Although I would not like to multiply wild textual conjectures, the present text in the MT needs some correction in order to be understood. The

---

25 See, e.g., Geertz, "Religion as a Cultural System"; Hargrove, *Sociology of Religion*; Smith, *Imagining Religion*; Asad, *Genealogies of Religion*; Bowie, *Anthropology of Religion*.
26 See Torrance, "Famous Saying"; Barstad, *Religious Polemics*, 113–114; Werner, "Micha 6,8"; Brueggemann, *Theology*, 460, 640; Carroll, "He has told you"; Hubbard, "Micah"; Ji, "Rhetorical Beauty"; Dreisbach, "Micah 6:8"; Brueggemann, "Walk Humbly"; Younan, "Do Justice"; Mostovicz and Kakabadse, "He has told you".
27 See, e.g., Jeppesen, "New Aspects"; Jeppesen, "Integrity"; Hillers, *Micah*,1–9; Kessler, *Micha*, 35–70; Andersen and Freedman, *Micah*, 3–29; Jacobs, "Bridging the Times"; Wöhrle, *Frühen Sammlungen*; Waltke, *Micah*, 1–16.

text itself starts from a description of a theophany, thence moving to a prophecy of doom containing threatening puns on place names. I read this chapter as a prophetic reflection on the sack of Samaria that hints at the inhabitants of Judah and Jerusalem, especially those who believe that the divine election has made them invulnerable to inimical threat.

In this chapter, a few polemic remarks on the religion can be found. Firstly in the beginning of the chapter:

> All this is for the rebellion of Jacob
>> And for the sins of the house of Israel.
> What is the rebellion of Jacob?
>> Is it not Samaria?
> What is the high place of Judah?
>> Is it not Jerusalem?[28]

This verse assesses the moral and religious conduct of both the Northern and the Southern Kingdom as trespassing the moral code. Words form the semantic field of 'sin' are applied: *peša'* and *ḥāṭā'*. The depreciating label *bāmāh*, 'high place', for the temple in Jerusalem indicates that the worship in this house of God was seen as illicit. Verse 5 is rather implicit on the character of this misconduct. The terminology is too general. In verse 7 the author is more explicit by referring to the 'idols'. This depreciating noun is polemic, since it assesses the veneration of divine – seen by the venerators as a worthy way of worship – as illicit.

3.2 Bad Conduct, Bad Prophecy, and Bad Idols (Micah 2–5)

The second part of the Book of Micah, chapters 2–5, is well known for its conceptual and compositional problems. In these chapters an interplay between prophecies of doom and prophecies of salvation can be found, as will be explained with the help of the example taken from the transition from Micah 3 to 4. Mic. 3,12 contains a fierce prophecy of doom:

> Zion will be ploughed like a field,
>> Jerusalem will become a pile of ruins.

Micah 4,1–4 is a vision full of hope with tones of peace and welfare. Micah 3,12 can be seen as an example of the end of time, foreshadowing doom and anxiety,

---

28 Mic. 1,5; Barstad, *Religious Polemics*, 184, correctly notes that this oracle is not directed towards Samaria, *pace* Fritz, "Wort"; Kessler, *Micha*, 187; see also Hillers, *Micah*, 16–21.

here the exile equals the eschaton, while Mic. 4,1–4 is written in the language of a consoling perspective of a salvific eschaton. What happened between the two chapters? How can both utterances be seen as part of the same text?

Here we meet the enigmatic alternation of the themes of "hope" and "doom" in Micah. This interchange has been interpreted in different ways. The classical, nineteenth-century exegesis and its aftermath have constructed a literary-critical or redaction-historical solution, as has been done for various other places in the prophets where the same problem occurs. Wellhausen has characterized this redaction in his diction that these later additions offered "Rosen und Lavendel statt Blut und Eisen."[29] In this view, Micah is seen as an eighth' century prophet of doom – compare Jer. 26 – but during or after the Babylonian exile the traditions relating to this prophet were augmented with optimistic phrases borrowed from the school of Deutero-Isaiah.[30] Other scholars read Micah, or at least Micah 2–5 as a coherent text.[31] Van der Woude, for example, has elaborated an ingenious theory.[32] In his opinion, chaps. 2–5 of the present Book of Micah contain the text of a dialogue between the pessimistic prophet and some optimistic pseudo-prophets. The views mentioned have strong and weak points. They are not convincing, however. So, I shall develop my own view taking into account the position of Hillers,[33] who characterizes Micah as "millenarian", or a prophet of a New Age. In Hillers' view, Micah foresees the coming of times of trouble before the onset of a golden Messianic age.[34]

Although van der Woude has given an interesting interpretation, I shall offer a different one: The prophet Micah had to bring a message of doom. This was necessary within the framework of his time, for the people of Israel had undermined their relationship with God, by transgressing the religious and social code implied in that relationship. At the same time, Micah knows about God's love and divine salvation. Both – doom and salvation – are brought together in a double-layered prophetic message. The first level is the prophecy of immediate doom as

---

29 Wellhausen, *Kleine Propheten*, 96.
30 Wellhausen, *Kleine PropheteI*, 142–43. See also, e.g., Jeremias, „Deutung"; Mays, *Micah*; Collins, *Mantle*, 72–73; Nogalski, *Literary Precursors*, 123–70; McKane, *Micah*, 17–19; Kessler, *Micha*, 41–47; Wagenaar, *Judgment and Salvation*, esp. 317–28; Jeremias, *Propheten*, 114–25.
31 E.g., Hagstrom, *Coherence*; Utzschneider, *Michas Reise*, 152–64; Dempsey, "Micah 2–3"; Wood, "Speech and Action"; Andersen, Freedman, *Micah*; Jacobs, *Conceptual Coherence*; Runions, *Changing Subjects*, 133–65; Bail, *"Verzogene Sehnsucht"*, 75–142; Smith-Christopher, "Refashioned Weapons", 186–209; Waltke, *Micah*, 143–342; Richelle, "Triptyque"; Wessels, "YHWH".
32 Van der Woude, 'Micah in Dispute', 244–60; Van der Woude, *Micha*, esp. 61–192; see also Boogaart, *Reflections on Restoration*, 49–88; Strydom, *Micah*, 127–57.
33 Hillers, *Micah* 4–8.
34 Hillers, *Micah* 6.

punishment. Doom, however, is not God's final word. In a more distant future Israel will be created anew within the dimensions of God's salvation. In order to describe this second level, Micah has borrowed the imagery of his great predecessor Isaiah.

In the meantime, a pattern has been developed that is characteristic of the prophetic futurology. This pattern might be called the "chastening pattern". Threat, conquest, downfall, exile, etc., are interpreted as divine acts in history. They are not, however, the end of time or history. Through the humiliation a new future is possible. This future can be reached by conversion,[35] or by new deeds of the deity, as the proclamation of Deutero-Isaiah. This pattern can be found, for instance in the Book of Consolation.[36]

Both in Micah and in Jeremiah a pattern can be detected.[37] In this prophetic view, history is the display of an interchange between "good times" and "bad times." The texts imply the idea that there is an alternation in time from periods of prosperity to times of trouble, and from situations of sorrow to periods of peace. Fear and freedom follow each other in a continuing interplay. This worldview can be characterized as proto-apocalyptic. In later apocalyptic literature, history is related in a schematic way. The past is presented in periods. I shall characterize this prophetic view as *proto*-apocalyptic since the concept of periodizing in its extreme form is not yet present. Besides, the active role of the divine being is stressed. I would add that a comparable worldview is attested in Mesopotamian texts that are roughly contemporaneous with "Micah." In the so-called Akkadian literary predictive texts the same pattern of interchange between "good times" and "bad times" is detectable.[38]

The theme of reversal is not only present in the Akkadian literary predictive texts, but also elsewhere in the ancient Near East. The hymn that was composed for the occasion of the coronation of the Neo-Assyrian king Assurbanipal is full of language and metaphors that express the traditional Mesopotamian view on the just king.[39] After the singing of this hymn, the king had to pronounce a blessing before Shamash – a blessing that recollects the themes from the loyalty oaths that Esarhaddon had concluded with his vassals shortly before his death and thus not long before Assurbanipal's inauguration. One of the lines reads:

---

35 As also in the theology of the Book of Kings; see, e.g., Nelson, *Historical Books*, 129–48; Römer, *So-called Deuteronomistic History.*
36 Becking, *Fear and Freedom.*
37 See also texts such as Amos 6,12; Jer. 2,32; 8,4; 18,14.
38 De Jong Ellis, "Observations"; Longman, *Akkadian Autobiography*; Neujahr, "Royal Ideology".
39 Arneth, „Möge Šamaš".

He who speaks with the king or treasonably,
if he is a notable, he will die a violent death;
if he is a rich man, he will become poor.[40]

Other texts in which this pattern can be detected are the Egyptian "Admonitions of Ipuwer" – from the First Intermediate Period[41] and the well-known Cyrus Cylinder.[42]

By viewing Micah 2–5 within this conceptual framework, a significant reading of the textual unit is evoked. To the author of the Book of Micah, the exile does not equal the eschaton. The forthcoming exiling of the inhabitants of Judah and the ruination of the city of Jerusalem – both took place some 125 years after the prophet Micah is generally assumed to have uttered his words – is not the end of history and certainly is not seen as the end of the divine involvement and support. This implies that a message can be read from the Book of Micah that is consoling for the *personae miserae* of all places and in all times.[43]

In this prophetic futurology some elements of religious polemics occur, mainly in the arguments justificating the forthcoming doom. I will discuss three of them.

3.2.1 Bad Conduct (Micah 2)

Micah's futurology is in conflict with the general ideas of his time. In his day and age society was on the move. From the archaeological evidence, in combination with the general knowledge on the Ancient Near East, the following picture emerges. On the level of *histoire conjoncturelle* a shift in the social organization in Ancient Israel is observable during Iron Age II. This shift basically is economic. The organization of the production of goods (e.g., food; clothing; tools) gradually changed from 'domestic' or 'kinship-related' into a more tributary system. In other words a situation in which they 'raised what they ate and they ate what they raised' changed into a production of surplus to satisfy the needs of a dominant ruling class that might have been subordinate to international power. A 'domestic' economy tends to be egalitarian, since that is an appropriate way to survive and to endure. Tributary societies are by implication non-egalitarian. A minority group is dominant over the society and wants to continue and extend its control. The shift from one form to the other has been provoked by the

---

40 SAA III 11: r. 9–10.
41 Ipuwer 8:1–5 (*COS* I, 96); Enmarch, *Ipuwer*.
42 See Kuhrt, "Cyrus Cylinder"; Van der Spek, "Cyrus the Great".
43 Kessler, *Micha*, 53–70.

contact that Israel had with competitive (e.g., Phoenicia and Syria) and dominant (Assyria) powers during Iron Age II.

As a result of this change a dichotomy in ancient Israelite society emerged. Some people profited from the economic prosperity, others however, suffered from the harsh side-effects of a market-oriented economy. Many fell into poverty. With his prophetic futurology Micah is reproaching this dichotomy. In the midst of 'modernity' he appeals to the traditional egalitarian social code. This is immediately clear from the opening stanza in Micah 2:

> Woe to those who scheme iniquity,
>> Who work out evil on their beds!
> When morning comes, they do it,
>> For it is in the power of their hands.
> They covet fields and then seize them,
>> And houses, and take them away.
> They rob a man and his house,
>> A man and his inheritance.[44]

At first sight, this prophecy of woe, does not contain elements of religious polemic: some persons are accused of wrong moral conduct. They are transgressing a part of the moral code that was originally based on an egalitarian principle: each person or family was allowed to have its own plot of land, the *naḥ^alā*. Lopsided growth leading to too great a difference was assumed to be restored by an act of compensation.[45] A distinction between 'moral code' and 'religion' is characteristic of a modern, Western, disenchanted view on reality. In our secular society we are accustomed, even required to separate the religious form the secular. However, there are strong indications that in the mind of the ancient Israelites, these dimensions were intertwined.[46] The Torah underlines time and again that there is no such thing as 'just' legal issues – matters of law are always bound up with the relationship with YHWH. In other words, the reproach on the moral conduct needs to be read as a form of religious polemic. Micah did disagree with the moral conduct of those who prospered while others became poor. To him, this conduct was not the correct expression of the Israelite religion.

---

[44] Mic. 2,1–2; see, e.g., Van der Woude, *Micha*, 65–69; Hillers, *Micah*, 31–33; Kessler, *Micha*, 111–19; Ben Zvi, "Wrongdoers"; Wagenaar, *Judgment and Salvation*, 208–220; De Moor, "Micah 2:1–13"; Nasuti, "Once and Future"; Jeremias, *Propheten*, 144–56.

[45] See, e.g., Deut. 15, 1 ff; Lev. 25.

[46] See, e.g., Stansell, *Micah and Isaiah*, 101–32; Otto, *Ethik*; Wagner, *Profanität und Sakralisierung*; Kratz, „Theologisierung"; Wells, "Cultic Versus the Forensic"; Miller, *Ten Commandments*, 1–9.

3.2.2 Bad Prophecy (Micah 3)

Prophecy has been an important means of divination in Ancient Israel.[47] In my view, religious specialists acted as consultants in and around the court advising indecisive or vacillating kings and magistrates.[48] About them Micah speaks the following words to the leaders of the nation:[49]

> Thus says YHWH concerning the prophets
> > Who lead my people astray;
> When they have something to bite with their teeth,
> > They cry, "Peace",
> But against him who puts nothing in their mouths,
> > They declare holy war.
> Therefore it will be night for you – without vision,
> > And darkness for you – without divination.
> The sun will go down on the prophets,
> > And the day will become dark over them.[50]

The identity of these 'prophets' is uncertain given the broad semantic spectre of the plural noun $n^eb\hat{i}\,\hat{i}m$ that as a container concept can refer to all sorts of religious specialists. They are portrayed by Micah as persons deceiving the people of Israel. Their main mistake – in his eyes – is their manipulating of the divine revelation. Next to that, their advice is dependant of what people are willing to pay them. The more you pay the nicer their prophecy. In times to come, however, these prophets will suffer from divine silence. The theme of prophetic silence functions as underpinning the very bitterness of Judah's fate. In days to come YHWH will leave his people, and the traditional channels of communication – divination and prophecy – will be closed. In the coming darkness YHWH will be out of reach; the people of Judah are left on their own.[51] The inability of a prophet to receive a vision on his behalf will deprive him of his last hope.

---

47 There is an abundance of literature on this topic; see, e.g., Barstad, "No Prophets?"; Cryer, *Divination*; Jeffers, *Magic and Divination*; Nissinen, "What is Prophecy?"; Becking, "Means of Revelation"; Stökl, *Prophecy*; Van der Toorn, "Turning Tradition".
48 See Benjamin, "Anthropology"; Becking, "Means of Revelation"; compare Walsh, *Scientists*.
49 See Mic. 3,1 and 9: 'heads (of the house) of Jacob and rulers of the house of Israel'.
50 Mic 3,5–6; see, e.g., Van der Woude, *Micha*, 106–117; Hillers, *Micah*, 44–46; Hagstrom, *Coherence*, 34–36; Carroll, "Night Without Vision"; Kessler, *Micha*,151–60; Jeremias, „Tradition und Redaktion"; Wagenaar, *Judgment and Salvation*, 245–47; Wood, "Speech and Action", 657–58; De Jong, *Isaiah*, 326; De Jong, "It Shall Be Night", 110–12.
51 The theme is also present in a lengthy letter written by Urad-Gula to an Assyrian king, SAA X 294: r. 30–33; see on this letter Nissinen, *References*, 84–88; Nissinen, *Prophets*, 158–63; and Becking, "Micah in Neo-Assyrian Light".

In a polemic note, Micah opposes himself to these prophets:

> On the other hand
>> I am filled with power ...[52]
>> And with justice and courage
> To make known to Jacob his rebellious act,
>> Even to Israel his sin.[53]

Over against the expedience and the self-interest of the prophets, stands Micah's obedience to Yʜwʜ. The proud and prestige, the arrogance and conceitedness are countered by an awareness of divine election. It is of course Micah's view and his depiction of himself as an almost perfect prophet that we encounter in the section. The polemic, however, is clear.[54]

3.2.3 Bad Icons (Micah 5)

The penultimate section in Micah's prophetic futurology is a prophecy of doom that is directed towards a complete dismantling of the vital structures of Judah and Jerusalem.[55]

> "In that day," declares Yʜwʜ,
> "I will destroy your horses from among you
>> and demolish your chariots.
> I will destroy the cities" of your land
>> and tear down all your strongholds.
> I will destroy your sorceries
>> and you will have no more fortune-tellers.
> I will destroy your idols
>> and your sacred stones from among you;
> you will no longer bow down
>> to the work of your hands.
> I will uproot from among you your Asherah poles
>> when I demolish your cities".[56]

---

52 The words *'èt rûaḥ yhwh*, 'which is the Spirit of Yʜwʜ', are to be seen as an explanatory gloss, see, e.g., Van der Woude, *Micha*, 116.
53 Mic. 3,8.
54 See esp. Stansell, *Micah and Isaiah*, 67–99.
55 Mic. 5,9–13; I construe Mic. 5,14 – But I will execute vengeance in anger and wrath on the nations which have not obeyed – as a word on the distant future in which Judah's fate will be restored by God's vengeance on the nations; see also the remarks by Kessler, *Micha*, 253.
56 Mic. 5,9–13; with, e.g., Willis, "Authenticity"; Hillers, *Micah*, 72–74; Jeppesen, "Micah v 13"; Kessler, *Micha*, 244–54.

The depiction of the power fabric is, however, not restricted to the features of the military. Jerusalem will be stripped off of its horses, chariots, and defensive strongholds. The forces on which the city and its elite based their confidence, will be disassembled. This act will eventually lead to the destruction of the city by foreign military forces. Another pillar of trust, however, will also be invalidated. In times to come, the leading elite can no longer rely on the religious elements of sorcery, idols, and the goddess Asherah. I will not discuss the phenomena in full, but only make a set of remarks.

Sorcery, *kesep*, refers here to the practice of consulting the dead ancestors in a situation of uncertainty. This divinatory form was widespread in Ancient Israel and in the ancient Near East.[57] In the Deuteronomistic code, this form of divination is strictly forbidden.[58] This code, however, was written about a century after Micah. Fortune-tellers, *me'onnîm*, were also practicing divination using the insights from astrology.[59] In the Deuteronomistic code, this form of divination is strictly forbidden.[60] This code, however, was written about a century after Micah. 'Idols' and 'sacred stones' were almost omnipresent in Iron Age Judah and Israel. They can be construed as part of the ancestor-religion, the images being the representation of the deceased ancestor who could be invoked for help and advice by bowing down before the image.[61] In the Deuteronomistic code, this form of divination is strictly forbidden.[62] This code, however, was written about a century after Micah.

The goddess Asherah, often represented by a pole, has in the Iron Age been the consort of Yhwh. Although some details of her veneration are still discussed – such as the connection with the plaque-figurines and the overlap with the veneration of goddesses such as Anat, Ishtar/Astarte, and the Queen of Heaven – Asherah can be construed as a *dea nutrix*. She was a protecting *dea nutrix* that could be evoked in times of danger and despair especially in the process of birth giving.[63] To the Deuteronomists the veneration of this goddess was seen as an illicit

---

57 See, e.g., Hillers, *Micah*, 73; Tsukimoto, *Untersuchungen zur Totenpflege*; Schmidt, *Israel's Beneficent Dead*; Pfälzner, "World of the Living"; Olyan, "Unnoticed Resonances"; Halton, "Allusions"; Mendez, *Condemnations*; Albertz, Schmitt, *Family and Household Religion*, 429–472.

58 See, e.g., Deut. 18,10, with 2 Kings 9,22; and Barstad, "Understanding"; Nicholson, "Deuteronomy 18.9–22".

59 See, e.g., Reiner, "Fortune-telling"; Bowen, "Daughters"; Cooley, "Story"; Maul, *Wahrsagekunst*.

60 See, e.g., Deut. 18,10; with Barstad, "Understanding".

61 There exists an abundance of literature on this topic. I confine myself to a few references: Mettinger, *No Graven Image*; Stavrakopoulou, *Land of Our Fathers*; Holter, "Bildeforbudet"; Albertz, Schmitt, *Family and Household Religion*, 74–171.

62 See, e.g., Deut. 4,16.23.25, with Deut. 27,15, 2 Kings 21,7.

63 See next to the literature from the 20th century CE, e.g., Dever, *Did God Have a Wife*; Becking, "Boundaries"; Gilmour, "Pictorial Inscription"; Pardee, "Many Faces"; Smith, "Blessing God"; Albertz, Schmitt, *Family and Household Religion*, 60–74

form of Yahwism.[64] This section in Micah 5 is obviously polemic. As ancestor to the Jahweh-Allein Bewegung, the prophet rebukes the religious trust of the Jerusalemite elite.

3.3 How to Appease an Angry God?

In the final chapters of the Book of Micah a different voice can be heard. Van der Woude's literary-critical division between 1–5 and 6–7 is still valid,[65] but I do not share his conclusion that Deutero-Micah should be depicted as a prophet from Northern Israel living before the fall of Samaria. I propose to read this pseudepigraphic text against a different historical background, namely that of the time of King Josiah. The text joins in the chorus of hope for the restoration of the Davidic dream of unity and for the return of the exiled Samarians. An interesting question would be, why were these chapters added to the book of Micah? My intuition would be that in circles of the Jahweh-Allein Bewegung the prophet Micah was claimed to be one of the important ancestors of the movement. The addition of the two pseudepigraphic chapters can then be seen as an appropriation to the period of transition from 'Manasseh' to 'Josiah'.

Micah 6,1–8 is an intriguing text in which this appropriation is easily detected. In the form of a judicial ordeal, the unit adapts various themes from Micah 2–5. Although the unit does not contain words from the semantic field of trespassing, the idea as such is clearly implied. Yhwh presents himself as the God who had guided the people of Israel through its darkest hours in history. This is apparent in his defence plea:

> Indeed, I brought you up from the land of Egypt and ransomed you from the house of slavery, and I sent before you Moses, Aaron, and Miriam. My people, remember now what Balak king of Moab counseled and what Balaam son of Beor answered him, *and* from Shittim to Gilgal.[66]

This historical retrospect refers to three important traditions. (1) The Exodus out of Egypt; (2) The inimical threat during the journey through the dessert,[67] and

---

64 See, e.g., Deut. 7,5; 12,3; 16,1; Judg. 6,25–30; 1 Kings 18,19; 2 Kings 17,16; with Park, "Cultic Identity".

65 Van der Woude, "Deutero-Micha"; his position is contested by all those scholars who operate with a redactionhistorical Dodekapropheton-theory. Interesting remarks can be found in Roth, *Israel und die Völker*, 172–232.

66 Mic. 6,5–6.

67 See Num. 22–24; see Schmidt, "Bileamüberlieferung".

(3) The conquest of the Holy Land.[68] This plea apparently evoked a consciousness of having failed among the people of Israel. They seek to appease the divine with excessive and almost impossible gifts: thousands of rams and even the life of the firstborn child. This merchandising proposal, however, is countered with an instruction that is much more human and humane:

> to do justice,
>> to love kindness,
>>> and to walk perceptively with your God.[69]

Historically, this shift in moral orientation coincides with the reformation in the times of Josiah.[70] I construe this reformation not only as a form of political power play on behalf of the newly formed priestly elite in Jerusalem, but also as an incentive to reframe the role of the cult in connection with appeasing the divine. Micah's saying then can be read as a polemic against all those who still believe in the power of excessive offerings.

4 Conclusion

According to Micah's programmatic name, the God of Israel is seen as incomparable to other divine beings. In the three sections of the book and during various stages of the composition of the Book of Micah, this concept of incomparability is spelled out, not a s a polemic against specific other deities, but as a rebuke against certain forms of Yahwism. This implies that the phrase 'Who is a God like Thee' in the doxology in Micah 7 should be interpreted in the framework of a *Religions interner Pluralismus*.[71] Within the variety of possible and existing Yahwisms, Micah – the prophet as well as the book – takes a specific and polemic stand.

---

68 Shittim was the last stopping place before the crossing of the Jordan (Josh. 3,1); Gilgal the first dwelling place in the promised land (Josh. 4,19). See, e.g., Van der Woude, *Micha*, 213; Andersen, Freedman, *Micah*, 523; Burnett, "Going Down".

69 Mic. 6,8; see Torrance, "Famous Saying"; Barstad, *Religious Polemics of Amos*, 113–114; Hillers, *Micah*, 75–79; Werner, "Micha 6,8"; Andersen, Freedman, *Micah*, 525–30; Carroll, "He has told you"; Kessler, *Micha*, 256–72; Dreisbach, "Micah 6:8"; De Moor, "Micah 6"; Jeremias, *Propheten*, 197–205; Decorzant, *Gericht*.

70 The historicity of the account in 2 Kings 22–23 is heavily debated; see, e.g., Lemche, "Reform"; Monroe, *Josiah's Reform*; Na'aman, "Discovered Book"; Albertz, "Deuteronomistic History"; Blenkinsopp, "Remembering Josiah". I have no space here to defend my somewhat obsolete view that at least some changes in the religious life of Ancient Israel took place some fifty years before the Babylonian Exile.

71 See Albertz, "Elterngebots"; Albertz, *Religionsgeschichte*; *pace* i.a. Peacock, "Who is a God like you?".

Das Gleichnis vom Frieden

Der Ort und die Funktion von Micha 4 in der Komposition
des Buches Micha

1 Ein schönes Bild

In seiner Studie über das Trostbüchlein Jeremias (Jer 30–31) vergleicht Christoph
Levin die Entdeckerarbeit eines Exegeten mit jemandem, der zufällig nicht durch
den üblichen Eingang einen Theatersaal betritt, sondern durch einen Seiteneingang plötzlich ins Theater kommt und von dieser Position aus einen ganz unerwarteten, neuen Blick auf das Schauspiel erlebt.[1] In diesem Beitrag möchte ich
gern einen unerwarteten Blick auf das Gleichnis vom Frieden in Mi 4 werfen und
verknüpfe dies mit der Hoffnung, dass es meinem Kollegen und langjährigen
Freund gefallen möge.

2 Das Theater

Zu den bekanntesten Texten der Bibel gehört die Vision des Propheten Micha
über die segensreiche und heilsame Zukunft der Welt:

1 Am Ende der Tage wird es geschehen:
     Der Berg des Hauses des HERRN steht fest gegründet
als höchster der Berge;
     er überragt alle Hügel. Zu ihm strömen Völker.
2 Viele Nationen gehen und sagen:
     Auf, wir ziehen hinauf zum Berg des HERRN
     und zum Haus des Gottes Jakobs.
     Er unterweise uns in seinen Wegen,
     auf seinen Pfaden wollen wir gehen.
     Denn von Zion zieht Weisung aus
     und das Wort des HERRN von Jerusalem.
3 Er wird Recht schaffen zwischen vielen Völkern
     und mächtige Nationen zurechtweisen bis in die Ferne.
Dann werden sie ihre Schwerter zu Pflugscharen umschmieden
     und ihre Lanzen zu Winzermessern.
Sie erheben nicht mehr das Schwert, Nation gegen Nation,
     und sie erlernen nicht mehr den Krieg.

---

1 Levin, *Verheißung*, 20.

https://doi.org/10.1515/9783111208657-008

> 4 Und ein jeder sitzt unter seinem Weinstock und unter seinem Feigenbaum
> und niemand schreckt ihn auf.
> Ja, der Mund des HERRN der Heerscharen hat gesprochen.
> 5 Auch wenn alle Völker ihren Weg gehen,
> ein jedes im Namen seines Gottes,
> so gehen wir schon jetzt im Namen des HERRN, unseres Gottes,
> für immer und ewig.[2]

Bekanntlich gibt es zwischen Mi 4 und Jes 2 auffallende Ähnlichkeiten. Die wissenschaftliche Diskussion zu diesem Punkt hat noch keinen Konsens gefunden. Die vier Möglichkeiten sind:

a. Mi 4 ist ursprünglich und wurde von Jesaja übernommen;
b. Jes 2 ist ursprünglich und wurde von Micha (oder den Herausgebern dieses Buches) entliehen;
c. beide haben eine bereits existierende Hymne der Jerusalemer Kulttradition entnommen;
d. der Text ist eine späte Interpolation in beiden Büchern.

Alle vier Modelle werden in den verschiedenen Kommentaren und Studien über Micha vertreten, wobei die Mehrheit sich für das letztgenannte entscheidet.[3] William McKane etwa hält die Einheit für eine nachexilische Einfügung in Micha und Jesaja.[4] Rainer Kessler vertritt die Entstehung des Textes aus der Micha-Tradition.[5] Nach Marvin Sweeney wurden die beiden Texte konstruiert, um verschiedene Stimmen in einer Debatte darzustellen, die darum kreiste, wie man mit der persischen imperialen Macht umgehen kann.[6] Dominic Rudman tendiert zu der Ansicht, dass das Buch Micha die ursprüngliche Form des Orakels enthalten hat.[7] Nach Adam van der Woude zitieren die optimistischen Gegner Michas hier Jesaja als Einwand gegen Michas Untergangsprophezeiung. Ihr Argument wäre: Man könne zwar Verhängnis und Exil prophezeien; der große Prophet Jesaja habe jedoch etwas anderes gesagt.[8] Van der Woudes Sichtweise ist zu einem gewissen Grad attraktiv, da er auf ein sehr frühes Beispiel des Missbrauchs der Schrift durch Zitieren hinweist. In meiner Wahrnehmung ist der Text im Micha-

---

2 Mi 4,1–5; *Einheitsübersetzung der Heiligen Schrift.*
3 Der Beschränkung wegen verzichte ich auf Vollständigkeit in den Anmerkungen.
4 McKane, *Micah*, 117–27.
5 Kessler, *Micha*, 178–81.
6 Sweeney, „Micah's Debate".
7 Rudman, „Zechariah 8:20–22".
8 Van der Woude, „Micah in Dispute"; Van der Woude, „Micah IV 1–5"; Van der Woude, *Micha*, 125–32.

buch ursprünglicher als im Jesajabuch.[9] Eines Tages fand ich indes einen Seiteneingang.

3 Der Seiteneingang

Einen unerwarteten Eingang entdeckte ich im Jeremiabuch. Innerhalb der größeren Einheit Jer 21,1–23,40 findet sich eine kurze Bemerkung. In Jer 21,1–23,40 sind Unheilsprophetien und Heilszusagen in Juxtaposition nebeneinandergestellt – ähnlich wie in Mi 2–5. In Jer 22,6–7 findet sich eine Unheilsankündigung für den König von Juda:

> Gilead warst du mir,
> der Gipfel des Libanon –
> fürwahr, ich mache dich zur Wüste,
> zu unbewohnten Städten.
> Ich biete Verwüster gegen dich auf,
> die mit ihren Äxten kommen,
> deine auserlesenen Zedern umhauen
> und ins Feuer werfen.[10]

Thematisch und im Bildregister ist dieser Text Mi 3,12 ähnlich. Auch jener Text – genau vor Mi 4,1 ff – redet über Vernichtung mit Bildern des Umsturzes, die aus landwirtschaftlichen Gegenden stammen. Anders als in Mi 4 folgt in Jer 22 keine Heilszusage, sondern eine Beschreibung der Folgen und Effekte des Umsturzes:

> Dann werden viele Völker an dieser Stadt vorübergehen und einander fragen:
> Warum hat der HERR so an dieser großen Stadt gehandelt?
> Und sie werden sagen:
> Weil sie den Bund mit dem HERRN, ihrem Gott, verlassen,
> sich vor anderen Göttern niedergeworfen und ihnen gedient haben.[11]

Es gibt eine wichtige intertextuelle Verknüpfung zwischen Mi 4,1–5 und diesem Text aus Jer 22:

Mi 4,2   Viele Nationen gehen und sagen [...]
Jer 22,8   Viele Völker werden an dieser Stadt vorübergehen [...] Und sie werden sagen:

---

9 Becking, „Religious Polemics".
10 Jer 22,6–7; see Lundbom, *Jeremiah 21–36*, 121–27; Mastnjak, *Deuteronomy*, 207–10.
11 Jer 22,8–9; siehe Lundbom, *Jeremiah 21–36*, 121–27; Mastnjak, *Deuteronomy*, 207–10.

Zwar sind unterschiedliche Verben gebraucht (הלך und עבר). Diese Zeitwörter gehören aber zum selben semantischen Feld. Beide zeichnen eine Bewegung in Richtung Jerusalems und evozieren das Bild einer Völkerwallfahrt. Der große Unterschied ist, dass in Micha die vielen Völker eine positive Bewegung nach Jerusalem machen, in Jeremia sind sie wegen des Schicksals Jerusalems in Erstaunen versetzt. Durch diesen geöffneten Seiteneingang kommt eine Frage auf: Wäre es möglich, dass Mi 4,2 – und auch Jes 2 – eine verwandelte Version von Jer 22,8 enthält?

4 Zwei Nebentüren

Um die Frage zu beantworten, sollen noch zwei andere Türen geöffnet werden. Nathan Mastnjak weist namentlich auf zwei Texte in der hebräischen Bibel hin, deren Thematik eng mit Jer 22,8 verbunden ist.[12] In einer Sammlung von Mahnworten im Buch Deuteronomium finden sich einige Verse, die die Folgen des von Israels Verfehlung verursachten Unheils plastisch schildern:

> [...] so werden alle Völker sagen:
>> Warum hat der HERR diesem Lande also getan?
>> Was ist das für ein so großer und grimmiger Zorn?
> So wird man sagen:
>> Darum, dass sie den Bund des HERRN, des Gottes ihrer Väter, verlassen haben, den er mit ihnen machte, da er sie aus Ägyptenland führte, und sind hingegangen und haben andern Göttern gedient und sie angebetet.[13]

Es gibt dabei zwei Unterschiede zu Jer 22. Erstens fehlt in Deut 29 ein Zeitwort der Bewegung, zweitens ist in diesem Text nicht die Rede von גוים רבים, ‚zahlreichen Völkern‘, sondern von כל רבים, ‚allen Völkern‘. Diese Beobachtung weist daraufhin, dass eine direkte literarische Entlehnung nicht wahrscheinlich ist. Meines Erachtens ist die Verbindung beider Texte ein Beispiel der Verarbeitung von Traditionsgut.

Etwas Vergleichbares muss gesagt werden über eine Passage in der Verheißung Gottes für Salomo nach dessen Tempelweihgebet.[14] Dieses Versprechen ist aber konditional. Es enthält eine Warnung, dass bei der Verfehlung des Volkes der Tempel zerstört werden soll.

---

12 Mastnjak, *Deuteronomy*, 207–10.
13 Deut 29,23–25; Mastnjak, *Deuteronomy*, 207–10.
14 1 Kön 8, siehe Talstra, *Solomon's Prayer*.

Dieses Haus wird zu einem Trümmerhaufen werden und jeder, der vorübergeht (עבר) wird sich entsetzen und zischen. Sie werden sagen (אמר):
Warum hat der HERR diesem Land und diesem Haus das angetan?
Und man wird antworten:
Weil sie den HERRN, ihren Gott, der ihre Väter aus Ägypten geführt hat, verlassen, sich an andere Götter gehängt, sich vor ihnen niedergeworfen und sie verehrt haben, darum hat der HERR all dieses Unglück über sie gebracht.[15]

In diesen Versen gibt es ein Zeitwort der Bewegung (עבר) die Völker sind aber reduziert auf einen amorphen כל, , jeder'.

Die Summe dieser Beobachtungen macht klar, dass es im alten Israel eine elastische Tradition gegeben hat, um die Reaktion unter den Völkern auf das negative Verhalten Israels zu beschreiben. Elemente dieser Tradition sind: ,Trümmerhaufen', das ,Vorbeigehen der Völker', das ,(fragende) Sprechen' und ,Israels Missachtung der Gebote des befreienden Gottes'. Mit dieser Tradition als Theaterglas möchte ich noch einmal die Bühne von Mi 4 betrachten.

5 Die Bühne: Micha 3,9–4,5

Wie ich schon früher argumentiert habe, soll Mi 3,9–4,5 in seiner Gesamtheit als Teil von Mi 2–5 gelesen werden.[16] Die scharfen Wechsel zwischen ,Heil' und ,Unheil' in Mi 2–5 lassen sich nicht mit einem literarkritischen oder redaktionsgeschichtlichen Modell erklären.[17] Die Versuche, das ganze Buch Micha als eine literarische Einheit zu lesen, sind aber auch nicht überzeugend.[18] Nach Adam van der Woude geben die Kapitel 2 bis 5 des vorliegenden Buches einen Dialog zwischen dem pessimistischen Propheten und einigen optimistischen Pseudo-Propheten wieder.[19] Diese Sicht überzeugt jedoch nicht. Vielmehr sollte auf der Sichtweise von Hillers aufgebaut werden, der Micha als Prophet eines neuen Zeitalters charakterisiert.[20]

---

15 1 Kön 9,8–9.
16 Becking, „Micah in Neo-Assyrian Light".
17 *Pace* Wellhausen, *Kleine Propheten*, 142–43; Jeremias, „Deutung"; Mays, *Micah*; Collins, *Mantle*, 72–73; Nogalski, *Literary Precursors*, 123– 170; McKane, *Micah*, 17–19; Kessler, *Micha*, 41–47; auch Schart, *Entstehung*; Ben Zvi, *Micah*; Wagenaar, *Judgement and Salvation*; Wöhrle, *Frühen Sammlungen*; Wöhrle, *Abschluss des Zwölfprophetenbuches*; Levin, „Vierprophetenbuch"; Zapff, „The Book of Micah".
18 *Pace* Hagstrom; Jacobs, *Conceptual Coherence*; LeCureux, *Thematic*; Cuffey, *Literary Coherence*.
19 Van der Woude, „Micah in Dispute"; Van der Woude, *Micha*, 61–192; siehe auch Boogaart, *Reflections on Restoration*, 49–88; Strydom, *Micah*, 127–57.
20 Hillers, *Micah*, 4–8.

Meines Erachtens präsentiert Mi 2–5 ein Muster, das für die prophetische Zukunftsschau charakteristisch ist. Dieses Muster könnte heißen: das Züchtigungsmuster. Bedrohung, Eroberung, Untergang, Exil usw. werden als göttliche Akte in der Geschichte interpretiert. Sie sind jedoch nicht das Ende der Zeit oder der Geschichte. Durch die Erniedrigung ist eine neue Zukunft möglich. In diesem Muster gibt es zwei Stufen der Zukunft:
- Ziemlich bald: die Zerstörung Jerusalems wegen ihrer Sünde;
- viel später – אחרית הימים, – ‚am Wendepunkt der Zeiten‘:[21] ein heilvoller Frieden ohne Ende.

Anders gesagt, der Text von Mi 2–5 sieht in der Zukunft ‚eine gute Zeit‘, aber erst nach einer ‚schlechten Zeit‘.

Mi 3,9–4,5 umfasst beide zeitlichen Dimensionen.[22] Mi 3,9–12 ist eine Ankündigung des Unheils, 4,1–5 ein Gleichnis vom Frieden. In Mi 3,9–4,5 sind die obengenannten Elemente der Tradition belegt – ‚Trümmerhaufen‘, das ‚Vorbeigehen der Völker‘, das ‚(fragende) Sprechen‘ und ‚Israels Missachtung der Gebote des befreienden Gottes‘. Sie haben in Micha aber einen anderen Platz und eine unterschiedliche Funktion als an den anderen Stellen:
- Das Element des ‚Vorbeigehens der Völker‘ wird noch am ähnlichsten gebraucht.
- Das ‚(fragende) Sprechen‘ hat aber eine ganz andere Funktion. Die Völker reden über Zion als den Mittelpunkt einer heilen Welt, in den sie einbezogen sein möchten.
- ‚Israels Missachtung der Gebote des befreienden Gottes‘ befindet sich im ersten Teil der Perikope. Das Thema gründet in der kommenden Zerstörung Jerusalems.
- Die ‚Trümmerhaufen‘ werden im ersten Teil der Perikope erwähnt. Performativ und literarisch haben sie eine andere Funktion als in den anderen Texten.

Sie werden nicht als Inhalt des Sehens oder des Fragens der Völker präsentiert. Die Völker prahlen nicht mit der Zerstörung. Erst nach der Wende אחרית הימים, ‚am Wendepunkt der Zeiten‘, nehmen die Völker Jerusalem wahr, dann aber als wiedererrichtete Stadt im Mittelpunkt der Welt. Diese Beobachtungen führen zu dem Schluss, dass Mi 3,9–4,5 als eine verwandelte Tradition zu lesen ist. Das traditionelle Mahnwort ist umgebogen zu einer Prophetie in zwei Stufen. Während in Jer 22, Dtn 29 und 1 Kön 9 die Trümmerhaufen das finale Schicksal Jerusa-

---

21 Z. B. Kosmala, „End of the Days"; Willis, „Expression"; Hillers, *Micah*, 50; Utzschneider. *Michas Reise*,152; Wagenaar, *Judgement and Salvation*, 28–31; Jacobs, *Conceptual Coherence*, 145.
22 Cuffey, *Literary Coherence*, 227–233, jedoch mit anderer Argumentation.

lems darstellen, sind sie in Micha nur eine Zwischenstation auf dem Weg zum unbeschränkten Frieden.

6 Der Schauspieler: Micha oder Jesaja?

Wer steht auf der Bühne? Anders gesagt: Ist das Gleichnis vom Frieden ursprünglicher in Micha oder in Jesaja? Um diese Frage zu beantworten, möchte ich einige Bemerkungen zu Jesaja 2,2–5 machen. Eine literarische Verbindung dieser Perikope mit dem vorangehenden Kapitel 1 – wie zwischen Mi 3,9–12 und 4,1–5 – ist nicht wahrscheinlich. Die beiden Kapitel gehören zu unterschiedlichen Texteinheiten.[23] Jes 1 ist zu interpretieren als das Präludium von Protojesaja oder des ganzen Buches in seinem finalen Entwurf, weil Jes 2 zur textlichen Einheit Jes 2–12 gehört, in der die Konfrontationen des Propheten mit König, Hof und Volk in neuassyrischer Zeit reflektiert sind. Das Thema der Trümmerhaufen wird in Jes 1 nur am Rande angedeutet:

> Doch Abtrünnige und Sünder brechen zusammen. Die den HERRN verlassen, sind am Ende. Denn sie werden zuschanden wegen der Eichen, die ihr begehrt habt, und ihr werdet beschämt wegen der Gärten, die ihr euch erwählt habt. Ja, ihr werdet wie eine Eiche, deren Blätter verwelken, und wie ein Garten, der kein Wasser hat. Dann wird der Starke zu Flachs und sein Tun zum zündenden Funken; beide verbrennen zusammen und keiner ist da, der löscht.[24]

Auch diese Passage verknüpft Unglaube und Untergang. Die Bilder sind aber einem anderen semantischen Feld entnommen wie in Mi 3. All diese Beobachtungen und Gedanken führen zu einer Hypothese über die Entstehung des Gleichnisses vom Frieden. Das Gleichnis ist zu erklären als Umwandlung einer Tradition über die Völker, die sich das Schicksal Israels ansehen. Da die Elemente dieser Tradition in Mi 3,9–4,5 enthalten sind, in Jes 2,2–5 aber nicht, ist es eher wahrscheinlich, dass der Autor von Jes 2–12 das Gleichnis aus dem Michabuch übernommen hat.

---

23 Siehe Williamson, *Isaiah 1–5*; Wilson, „Isaiah 1–12“.
24 Jes 1,28–31.

Israel and the Nations in the Book of Micah

1 Introduction

The Book of Micah[1] is a rich but complex composition. Its seven chapters contain beautiful language, catching metaphors and theological depth. Meanwhile the debate on origin, emergence and composition of this book has not reached a scholarly consensus. Various positions are defended: from full authenticity in the eighth century BCE to a fragmented redaction history ending in a *dodekapropheton*-redaction in the Hellenistic era. I will add my own proposal later. When it comes to the theme of this session, it should be noted that both Israel and the Nations are depicted differently throughout the Book of Micah. Israel is seen both as the object of divine wrath and punishment and as the object of divine love and grace. The Nations are at some instances cast in the role of the executors of divine wrath. In other texts, however, they are depicted as coming to Jerusalem to seek God and his justice. I will discuss a few instances within the parameters of what I construe to be the design of this prophetic book:
- Micah 1   An original, but distorted prophecy
- Micah 2–5   A prophetic futurology based on a variety of reworked sayings from the Micah-tradition
- Micah 6–7   A Josianic treatise based on pseudepigraphy

2 Micah 1: An Original, but Distorted Prophecy

The first chapter of the Book of Micah – in its Masoretic version – seems to be in disorder. Several proposals have been made to reconstruct a more original or fluid text form. Although, I would not like to elaborate wild textual conjectures, the present text in the MT needs some correction in order to be understood. The text itself starts from a description of a theophany moving to a prophecy of doom containing threatening puns on place names. I read this chapter as a prophetic reflection on the sack of Samaria, that is hinted at the inhabitants of Judah and Jerusalem, especially to those who belief that the divine election have made them invulnerable for inimical threat.

---

1 Text of a paper presented at the SBL Annual Meeting in Atlanta, 2010. Footnotes are given sparingly.

https://doi.org/10.1515/9783111208657-009

2.1 Israel in Micah 1

In this first chapter, the theophany is directed to a prophecy of judgment for Israel:

> For I will make Samaria a heap of ruins in the open country, planting places for a vineyard. I will pour her stones down into the valley, and will lay bare her foundations. (Mic 1:6 NAS)

The prophet will mourn for this disaster:

> Because of this I must lament and wail I must go barefoot and naked; I must make a lament like the jackals. And a mourning like the ostriches. (Mic 1:8 NAS)

This mourning is exemplified in the lament containing puns on the names of Judahite cities in villages (Mic. 1,10–16)

2.2 The Nations in Micah 1

In the same chapter, the nations are summoned to act as witnesses on the judgement for Israel:

> Hear, O peoples, all of you; Listen, O earth and all it contains, and let the Lord God be a witness against you, The Lord from His holy temple. (Mic 1:2 NAS)

Although not indicated as such, the nations are seen as the executors of divine punishment in, for instance in 1,15:

> Moreover, I will bring on you the one who takes possession, O inhabitant of Mareshah. The glory of Israel will enter Adullam. (Mic 1:15 NAS)

2.3 Israel and the Nations in Micah 1

In this first section an overtly clear image on the connection between Israel and the Nations becomes clear. Israel has trespassed and will be punished by God using the Nations as the instrument of his wrath. Here the author is using a traditional antagonistic pattern to cope with the reality of his days.

3 A Prophetic Futurology

3.1 Introduction to Micah 2–5

The second part of the Book of Micah, 2–5, is well known for its conceptual and compositional problems. In these chapters an interplay between prophecies of doom and prophecies of salvation can be found. This interchange has been interpreted in different ways. The classical, nineteenth century exegesis and its aftermath have constructed a literary-critical or redaction-historical solution as has been done at various instances in the prophets where the same problem occurs. Wellhausen has depicted the pattern of this redaction in saying that these later redactions offered "Rosen und Lavendel statt Blut und Eisen".[2] In this view Micah is to be seen as an eighth century prophet of doom – compare Jer. 26 – but during or after the Babylonian exile the traditions on this prophet were enlarged with optimistic phrases borrowed from the school of DtIsa. Some scholars read Micah, or at least Mi. 2–5 as a coherent text. Van der Woude has elaborated an ingenious theory. In his opinion the chapters 2 to 5 of the present Book of Micah contain the text of a dialogue between the pessimistic prophet and some optimistic pseudo-prophets. All views mentioned have strong and weak points. They are not convincing, however. My own view takes into account the position of Hillers who characterizes Micah as 'millenarian', or a prophet of a New Age. In Hillers' view Micah foresees the coming of times of trouble before the onset of a golden Messianic age. I will return to this problem after having a look at the texts.

3.2 Israel in Micah 2–5

Micah 2–5 starts with a woe-oracle that announces doom for a specific group within Israel, namely those who profited from the economic situation at the expense of the poor and the needy (Mic. 2,1–5):

> Therefore, thus says the LORD, "Behold, I am planning against this family a calamity from which you cannot remove your necks; and you will not walk haughtily, for it will be an evil time." (Mic 2:3 NAS)

The theme of economic transgressions is taken up in Mic 2,8–9 leading to a prophecy that foresees exile:

---

2 Wellhausen, *Kleine Propheten*, 96.

> Arise and go, for this is no place of rest. Because of the uncleanness that brings on destruction, a painful destruction. (Mic 2:10 NAS).

Beyond exile there is hope for return:

> I will surely assemble, O Jacob, all of thee; I will surely gather the remnant of Israel (Mic 2:12 KJV)

Note, however, that this prophecy of salvation is only directed to the 'remnant of Israel', that is a smaller group within the community that does not coincide with those to whom the woe-oracle was addressed. The remnant will be liberated by the acts of a specific character the הַפֹּרֵץ, 'breaker':

> The breaker goes up before them; they break out, pass through the gate, and go out by it. So their king goes on before them, And the LORD at their head. (Mic 2:13 NAS)

Micah 3,1 ff continues the theme of social injustice by a specific group within Israel, where the leaders of the nation are addressed and reproached:

> You who hate good and love evil, who tear off their skin from them and their flesh from their bones. (Mic 3:2 NAS)

Their conduct will lead to doom that cannot be hold or set at peace by the intervention of all sorts of diviners and religious specialists, since they will be unable to hear from the divine in the moment of disaster (Mic 3,5–8). This theme is continued in Micah 3,9–12. That unit, again, states that the trespasses of the Jerusalemite elite will lead to ruination of Zion and Jerusalem.

From Micah 4 a different image arises:

> In days to come
> > the mountain where the temple stands
> will be the highest one of all,
> > towering above all the hills.
> Many nations will come streaming to it,
> > and their people will say:
> "Let us go up the hill of YHWH
> > to the temple of Israel's God.
> For He will teach us what He wants us to do;
> > we will walk in the paths he has chosen.
> For YHWH's teaching comes from Jerusalem;
> > from Zion He speaks to His people".
> He will settle disputes among the nations,
> > among the great powers near and far.

> They will hammer their swords into hoes
>> and their spears into pruning-knives.
> Nations will never again go to war,
>> never prepare for battle again.
> Everyone will live in peace
>> among his own vineyards and fig-trees,
> and no one will make him afraid
>> YHWH almighty has promised this.

Jerusalem is no longer ruined waste land, but in sense the *navel* of the world. Israel will live peacefully and unstartled. It is an interesting question to discuss whether the pronoun 'everyone' refers to the whole of Israel or to a smaller more specific group. In my opinion, the rest of Micah 4 hints at an interpretation that only a group within Israel is referred to that does not coincide with the leaders etc. mentioned and reproached in Micah 2–3. In Micah 4,6–7 I read:

> "In that day," declares the LORD, "I will assemble the lame, And gather the outcasts, Even those whom I have afflicted. I will make the lame a remnant, And the outcasts a strong nation, And the LORD will reign over them in Mount Zion From now on and forever." (Mic 4:6–7 NAS)

Micah 4,8–13 is a rather enigmatic text and quite difficult to construe. If we take this unit to be an authentic part of Micah 2–5, it is very difficult to connect it conceptually with the other units within Micah 2–5. In Micah 4,8–14, Babylon – and not Assur – is mentioned. Israel is promised to pulverise many nations. Reading the unit, I get the impression that salvation does not lay in a return from exile, but in going into exile. Therefore, I tend to see Micah 4,8–13 as a later interpolation.

Micah 5,1–6 in a way repeats the themes from Micah 4. A few remarks. The liberator referred to in Mic. 5,2:

> From you One will go forth for Me to be ruler in Israel. (Mic 5:2 NAS)

He is like the 'breaker' in Mic. 2 a representative of the typos of the *Heilszeitherrscher* known form Ancient Near Eastern proto-apocalyptic speculations on history as an interchange between 'good times' and 'bad times'. This 'ruler' will in times to come shepherd over the remnant of Israel:

> Then the remnant of Jacob Will be among many peoples Like dew from the LORD, Like showers on vegetation Which do not wait for man Or delay for the sons of men. (Mic 5:7 NAS)

I construe the 'remnant of Jacob' to refer to that part of Israel that formerly had been oppressed by the elite and that after a period of sorrow and exile will be gathered into a new existence by the 'ruler'.

Micah 5,9–14 is to be seen as a prophecy of doom in which – comparable to some units in Micah 2 and 3 – the elite will be punished for their trespasses. Interestingly, the focus in this unit is not so much on social injustice as well as on religious misdeeds, as is implied in:

> I will cut off your carved images And your *sacred* pillars from among you, So that you will no longer bow down To the work of your hands. (Mic 5:13 NAS)

It should be note, however, that a split between social injustice and religious misbehaviour is a typical post-enlightenment classification of whom the ancient Israelites probably were not aware.

3.3 The Nations in Micah 2–5

In the prophecies of doom and disaster in Micah 2 and 3, the nations are not referred to explicitly. In the culmination of these prophetic sayings, however, an interesting *passivum* occurs:

> Therefore, on account of you, Zion will be plowed as a field, Jerusalem will become a heap of ruins, And the mountain of the temple *will become* high places of a forest. (Mic 3:12 NAS)

The verb form תֵּחָרֵשׁ, 'will be ploughed', is to be construed as a passive voice, a Niph'al. The subject of the act of ploughing, however, is silenced by the use of the passive form and it is up to the reader to fill in this syntactical empty space. A comparable remark could be made about the syntagma הָיָה לְ, 'will become' in the second line of this verse. From the co-text and the context of Micah 2–3 this empty space could only be filled with an unspecific *agent*. The actual name of the 'other nation' is less important than its role as executor of divine wrath.

In the prophecy of hope in Micah 4,1–4, the nations play a quite different role. They no longer are approaching Jerusalem as agents of wrath, but as seekers of peace and divine instruction.

In the enigmatic unit Micah 4,8–14, the nations play again another role.

> Arise and thresh, daughter of Zion, For your horn I will make iron. And your hoofs I will make bronze, That you may pulverize many peoples, That you may devote to the LORD their unjust gain And their wealth to the Lord of all the earth. (Mic 4:13 NAS)

The nations are now seen as the object of revenge since they will be crunched by a very powerful Israel. In the final unit, Micah 5,9–14, the nations are again cast in the role of the instrument of wrath.

3.4 Israel and the Nations in Micah 2–5

Reading Micah 2–5 at face value, we are left with a complex and confusing image of different roles and changing depictions. They run parallel to the interchange of doom and hope. As referred to above, these anomalies have often been solved by assuming a process of redaction of the text of Micah in various stages. I would like to embark on a different solution. That I present in the following graph:

	Immediate Future	Later Future
Israel	The leaders will be punished for their deeds	The remnant will be saved and gathered
Nations	Will be an instrument of divine wrath and revenge	Will take part in the salvation of Israel

In doing so, I assume that Micah 2–5 is speaking about two types of future. In the near future a turn in the sense of a decisive change will take place. *bᵉʾaḥrît hayyāmmîm* refers to a decisive turn in time, but not the end of time, rather the end of a period and the beginning of a new one. The salvation described in Micah 2–5 is hoped to take place in a more distant the future, but within the limits of time and Israelite history after the people went through a period of chastening.

4 Micah 6–7

4.1 Introduction to Micah 6–7

In the final chapters of the Book of Micah a different voice can be heard. Van der Woude's literary-critical division between (1)2–5 and 6–7 is still valid, but I do not share his conclusion that Deutero-Micah should be depicted as a prophet from Northern Israel living before the fall of Samaria. I propose to read this pseudepigraphic text against a different historical horizon, namely that of the times of King Josiah. This date is underscored by the presence of proto-deuteronomistic language and theology in Micah 6–7. In that time frame, the text shares the choir of hope for restoration of the Davidic dream of unity and for return of the exiled Samarians. An interesting question would be, why these chapters were added to the book of Micah? As yet, I don't have an answer to that question.

4.2 Israel in Micah 6–7

In the 'covenant'-lawsuit Mic. 6,1–8 it is only Israel that is addressed or referred to. Israel is indirectly reproached for their disobedience to YHWH who is portrayed here as the God that guided them through history. The way to salvation in this text is impressive. Remission cannot be reached by an abundance of offerings but only:

> [...] to do justice, to love kindness, and to behave prudently by walking with your God. (Mic 6,8)

The unit Micah 6,9–16 is quite enigmatic and contains a variety of exegetical riddles that will not be discussed here. The unit starts with an appeal to an unnamed city:

> The voice of the LORD will call to the city.
>   And it is sound wisdom to fear Thy name:
> "Listen to the rod
>   and to who has appointed it" (Mic 6:9)

The elite of this city is reproached for its social injustice and its religious misbehavior. Their deeds and doings are construed as a continuation of the acts of the house of Omri. Omri and Ahab function as arch-villains. The unnamed city will be punished. For the description of the character of the doom language from the ancient Near Eastern vassal treaties and loyalty-oaths – and by implication from Deuteronomy 28 – is adopted. This is apparent in the futility-curses:

> You will eat,
>   but you will not be satisfied,
>   And your vileness will be in your midst.
> You will *try* to remove *for safekeeping*,
>   But you will not preserve *anything*,
> And what you do preserve
>   I will give to the sword.
> You will sow but
>   you will not reap.
> You will tread the olive but
>   will not anoint yourself with oil;
> And the grapes,
>   but you will not drink wine. (Mic. 6,14–15)

The woe-oracle Mic. 7,1–6 depicts in its indictment the situation of despair in which the prophet lives. The language in this unit can be labeled by using the word 'absent'. The line 'there is no grape to eat' stands symbolic for the absence of piety, love and solidarity in Israel. Note that the language here resembles the description of a 'bad time' or a world turned topsy-turvy as in the Accadian literary predictive texts.

Micah 7,11–13 contains a prophecy of hope on the return from exile and diaspora. Israel will in days to come return to its own land. This theme is continued in the next unit.

4.3 The Nations in Micah 6–7

In the 'covenant'-lawsuit Mic. 6,1–8 the nations are absent. In the next section, Mic. 6,9–16, they seem to be absent. Much depends on the interpretation of the word *maṭṭèh* in verse 9. I still construe the word as meaning 'rod' and interpret the context – in parallelism with Isa. 10 – as another example of the nations being the instrument of divine wrath. In the woe-oracle 7,1–6 the nations are absent. The prophecy of hope for Israel, Mic. 7,11–13, turns out to be a prophecy of doom for the nations, although they are not mentioned as such:

> And the earth will become desolate because of her inhabitants,
>> On account of the fruit of their deeds. (Mic. 7:13 NAS)

The harshness is slightly softened in the following prophecy of hope for Israel. The fate of the nations in those days to come is not death or desolation but humiliation leading to veneration of the God of Israel:

> Nations will see and be ashamed Of all their might. They will put *their* hand on *their* mouth, Their ears will be deaf. They will lick the dust like a serpent, Like reptiles of the earth. They will come trembling out of their fortresses; To the LORD our God they will come in dread, And they will be afraid before Thee. (Mic. 7:16–17 NAS)

4.4 Israel and the Nations in Micah 6–7

In the final part of the Book of Micah there are two different concepts on the connection between Israel and the nations to be detected. (a) The view that the nations will act out the divine wrath as a rod. (b) The view that in the end the nations will be humiliated while Israel is revived.

5 Conclusion

In the Book of Micah various ideas on Israel and the nations as well on their connection are expressed. The differences can be clarified by assuming redaction-historical division into three sections and by construing the middle part of the book as a prophetic futurology that talks about two different futures: an imminent and more eschatological. By way of final remark: The authors of this book are mostly concerned with the fate of Israel. The nations do not play the main part, but they act or will act in the various roles as instruments of the divine love for this specific nation. Even in the prophecies of doom God is to be seen as acting on behalf of the real interest of Israel.

'Who does not make firm his anger forever?'

Bodily Metaphors for Yʜwʜ in Micah 6–7

1 Introduction

To state that the Book of Micah is complicated and not-easily understood is more than a truism.[1] Many features, the interchange between doom and salvation, the function of the text within the Book of the Twelve, to name but two topics, are continually debated among scholars without a consensus rising at the horizon. I will not describe or summarize these debates. That would break the limits of this contribution.

I just plunge in by stating that I adopt and adhere the view firstly phrased by Burkitt. According to him – and many others – chapters 6–7 of the Book of Micah need to be disembedded from the first five chapters of that book.[2] In line with his view, I propose to read Deutero-Micah as text written against a different historical horizon than Micah 1–5. With Micah 6–7, we are in the times just before the reign of King Josiah and the reformation of the cult inspired by the finding of a law-book in the temple of Jerusalem. The unit 6–7 shares the choir of hope for restoration of the Davidic dream of unity and for return of the exiled Samarians and is clearly connected to the Yahweh-alone movement. The argument for this view is well-known and – in my view – convincing. Differences at the level of words and phrases, topographical and historical allusions, as well of a conceptual character separate 6–7 from (1)2–5.

Nevertheless, Juan Cruz argued in his 2016 monograph *"Who is Like Yahweh?"* against this view.[3] In his opinion, the legal metaphors in Micah 6:1–16 as well as the pastoral imaginary in Micah 7:7–14 are similar to the legal and pastoral metaphors in Micah 1–5. To him this is an argument for the literary coherence of the book of Micah. His view induced me to rethink the literary-critical matter.

At first sight, Cruz seems to be correct. As for the pastoral metaphors, nouns like ṣo'n, 'flock', and šeʾērît, 'remnant', appear in both sections:

---

1 Paper presented at the EABS meeting, Warsaw 2019. Footnotes are reduced in number.
2 Burkitt, "Micah 6 and 7".
3 Cruz, *Who is like Yahweh?*.

https://doi.org/10.1515/9783111208657-010

1–5	ṣo'n, flock	Mi 2:12	כְּצֹאן בָּצְרָה	I will bring them together like sheep in a pen, like a flock in its pasture; the place will throng with people.
		Mi 5:7	בְּעֶדְרֵי־צֹאן	The remnant of Jacob will be among the nations, in the midst of many peoples, like a lion among the beasts of the forest, like a young lion among flocks of sheep,
6–7		Mi 7:14	צֹאן נַחֲלָתֶךָ	Shepherd your people with your staff, the flock of your inheritance,

The same is true for the legal metaphors in chapters 1 and 6. His view, however, is not convincing for three reasons.

2 Too General a Field of Reference

The legal metaphors in chapters 1 and 6 are of too general a character. The so-called *rîb*-pattern is attested throughout the Hebrew Bible and in a variety of literary forms.[4] At times the verb *rîb* refers to a quarrel between human beings/groups. See for instance:

– Gen. 13:7   And there was strife between the herdsmen of Abram's livestock and the herdsmen of Lot's livestock.

In other texts the verb refers to the act of a human judicial ordeal:

– Deut. 21:5   The Levitical priests shall step forward, for the LORD your God has chosen them to minister and to pronounce blessings in the name of the LORD and to decide all cases of dispute and assault.

These texts – and others such as Exodus 17:7; Judges 12:2; 2 Sam 15:2; Jer. 15:10; Ezek. 44:24 – refer to human quarrel and strife, sometimes with a legal dimension that functioned as the tenor for the metaphor in which a defective relationship between God and human is depicted: YHWH quarrels with his people:

– Jer. 25:31   'A clamor has come to the end of the earth, Because the LORD has a controversy with the nations. He is entering into judgment with all flesh;

---

4 See Nielsen, *Prosecutor and Judge*.

As for the wicked, He has given them to the sword,' declares the Lord."[5]

In sum: the presence of legal metaphors in both Micah 1 and 6 cannot be seen as an argument for common authorship.

3 Varying Functions of the Metaphor

Every metaphor is embedded in a broader context of communication. This implies that, although a specific noun is present in two or more cases, the contextual function of the figurative language can differ. The metaphor YHWH = Judge, for instance, functions differently in varying contexts. In an oracle of doom this metaphor functions as an indication that punishment on Israel and the downfall of the land are the outcome of a divine judicial verdict. In the context of a prophecy of salvation, the same metaphor functions as an indication that the liberation of Israel and the downfall of its enemies are the outcome of a divine judicial verdict.

The question is, whether this difference is applicable to the metaphors in Micah. I will examine here the pastoral metaphor only. In Micha 2:12 the noun ṣo'n, 'flock', refers to 'Israel' in the despair of the diaspora:

12 I will certainly collect you completely, Jacob,
    I will certainly gather the remnant of Israel,
  I will put them unitedly like sheep in an enclosure.
    Like a flock in the midst of its pasture.
  They will be noisy with man.
13 The one who made a breach goes up before them.
    They break through, pass the gate,
        and go out through it.
  Their king will pass through before them
    YHWH in front of them.[6]

In this context, the pastoral metaphor communicates the gathering of 'Israel' in the save haven of an enclosure, from which they will go out to return to their homeland.

---

5 See also Jer. 50:34; Hosea 4:1.
6 Micah 2:12–13.

Micah 5:7 is part of a prophecy proclaiming an unexpected change:

6 The remainder of Jacob will be in the middle of great nations
    like dew from YHWH,
        like abundant rain on vegetation
    that does not wait for a man,
        or bide for mankind.
7 The remainder of Jacob will be in the middle of great nations
    will be like a lion among the animals of the forest
        like a young lion among the flock of sheep,
    that when he passes by tramples
        and devours while no-one will be saved.
8 She will raise her hand against her enemies
    and all your enemies will be cut off.[7]

'Israel' in the despair of the diaspora will be transformed into fierce force. Like a lion the remnant will rule over its enemies. This, obviously, is a different role than that of a flock under divine guidance in Micah 2 and therefore cannot be used as an argument for common authorship.

In Micah 7:14, these two roles are combined in a different frame.

14 Shepherd your people with you staff
        – the flock of your inheritance –
    That dwells in isolation in a forest
        in the middle of an orchard.
    They will pasture in Bashan and Gilead
        as in the eternal days.
15 As in the days of your going out of the land of Egypt
        I will show him wonders.
16 The nations will see and be ashamed
        despite of all their strength.
    They shall put hand to mouth,
        their ears will be deafened.
17 They will lick dust like a serpent
        Like reptiles of the earth they will quake out of their dungeons.[8]

This unit makes a distinction within Israel between 'shepherd' and 'flock'. The shepherd – standing for the new ruler – is summoned to lead and guide the flock (// 2:12) putting the 'enemies' to shame (// 5:6 ff). By putting the staff of the shepherd into human hands the ruling role of God is converted into human reign. This observation too makes a common authorship of the various chapters in the book of Micah less likely.

---

7 Micah 5:6–8.
8 Micah 7:14–17.

As for the pastoral metaphor, a difference in function within the Book of Micah can be detected. It is my conviction that a comparable difference is present in the other metaphors.

4 Variety in Root-Metaphors

It is my conviction that there is a difference in the image of God between the two (or three) parts of the book of Micah. The first five chapters of the Book of Micah present God as a character that speaks and acts. In the final two chapters, the language on God is deepened. YHWH is depicted as a divine being with all sorts of emotions varying between anger and comfort. This statement is in need of a substantiation. I therefore will scan the Book of Micah for its language describing the acts of God.

Micah 1

1:2	Be a witness	hāyāh leʿēd	
1:3	To come; go out	yāṣāh	epiphany
1:3	To descend	yārad	epiphany
1:3	To tread	dārak	epiphany
1:6	I will set Samaria to a heap of stones in the field	śîm	judgment
1:6	I will hurl down her stones to the valley	nāgar	judgment
1:7	I will set all her idols to devastation	śîm	judgment
1:15	I will bring a conqueror over you	bôʾ	judgment

Micah 2

2:3	I will devise an evil against this clan	ḥāšab rāʿā	judgment
2:12	To collect	ʾāsap	salvation
2:12	To gather	qābaṣ	salvation
2:12	I will put them unitedly like sheep in an enclosure	śîm	salvation
2:13	To go in front	ʿābar	salvation

Micah 3

3:4	but he will not answer them	*lo' 'ānāh*	judgment
3:4	he will conceal his face for them	*sātar pānîm*	judgment
3:5	To speak	*'āmar*	judgment
3:7	no answer will come from God		judgment

Micah 4

4:2	To teach (good ways)	*yārāh*	salvation
4:3	He will settle disputes between the nations	*šāpaṭ*	salvation
4:6	To collect	*'āsap*	salvation
4:6	To gather	*qābaṣ*	salvation
4:7	I will set the lame as a remnant	*śîm*	salvation
4:7	To reign	*mālak*	salvation
4:10	There [= Babylon], Yнwн will redeem you from the hand of your enemies!	*gā'al*	salvation
4:12	To gather	*qābaṣ*	judgment

Micah 5

5:9	To cut off	*kārat*	salvation
5:9	To destroy	*'ābad*	salvation
5:10	To cut off	*kārat*	salvation
5:10	To demolish	*hāras*	salvation
5:11	To cut off	*kārat*	salvation
5:12	To cut off	*kārat*	salvation
5:13	To pull out	*nātaš*	salvation
5:13	To exterminate	*šāmad*	salvation
5:14	To take revenge	*nāqam*	salvation

All these divine acts are presented as a divine reaction to the trespasses of Judah and Jerusalem. They are seen as God's way to set things right. God's deeds and doings against the 'other nations' are not motivated. There is no inner motivation narrated. Neither divine anger nor divine love are presented as the source of God's acts that will lead to salvation for Israel.

There are a few traces of emotive language in Micah 1–5. In 1:8, language of mourning is present:

> 8 Because of this, I will mourn,
>   and howl,
>   and go barefoot
>   and naked,
>   I will make a wailing like the jackals
>   and mourning like the daughters of an ostrich.

The 'I' in this lament should be interpreted as the prophetic, not as the divine 'I'. This view is in need of an argument. Elsewhere in the Book of Micah the 'I' can be seen as referring to Yнwн. This opens the lane to construe the 'I' in 1:8 as referring to Yнwн.[9] In Micah 7:8–9 a prophetic 'I' longs for the future. In that section the 'I' is inclusive, since it refers to those in Judah and Jerusalem who were punished by the divine wrath. In Micah 1:8, 'I' refers to a prophetic figure who is emotionally upset about the impending fate of his people. This prophetic 'I' is presented not as an unmoved messenger, but as a person suffering the fate he announces.[10]

In 2:7 God is seen as impatient:[11]

> 2:7 May that be proclaimed, house of Jacob?
>   Is the spirit of Yнwн that impatient?
>   Are these his doings?

Here, however, the image of god among the ruling elite as argument against the impending judgement is focalized by the author/redactor. The 'accused' accuse Micah for denying the divine predicate of being *'èrèk 'appayim*, 'long-suffering'.[12]

In Micah 3, God is portrayed in bodily language

---

9 Thus for instance Runions, *Changing Subjects*, 125.
10 Cruz, *Who is like Yahweh?*, 103–07.
11 The verb *qāṣar*, 'to be short', with the noun *rûaḥ* forms the idiomatic expression 'to be impatient' (see also Job 21:4).
12 See, e.g., Exod. 34:6.

3:4   but he will not answer them.
       he will conceal his face for them.
3:7   since no answer will come from God.

These depictions of God, however, should be construed as signs of absence of empathy.

The only instance where God is seen as steered by emotions is found in the final verse of chapter 5:

5:14   I will take vengeance in anger and fury
       on the people who did not listen.

I will come back to this verse later.

The language of divine action – present in Micah 1–5 – continues in Micah 6 and 7:

Micah 6			
6:1	To speak	'*āmar*	
6:2	To dispute	*yākaḥ*	
6:4	Brought up	'*ālāh* Hif.	past
6:4	To ransom	*pādāh*	past
6:4	I have sent before you Moses, Aaron, and Miriam	*šālaḥ*	past
6:8	To tell	*nāgad*	past
6:13	To make ill	*ḥālāh* Hif	future
6:13	To smite	*nākāh*	future
6:16	I will make you an object of horror	*nātan*	future

Micah 7			
7:9	To dispute (my dispute)	*rîb*	future
7:9	To execute justice	'*āśāh mišpaṭ*	future
7:9	He will bring me out to the light	*yāṣāh*	future

These two chapters, however, are larded with language in which Yhwh is depicted as a divine being with all sorts of emotions varying between anger and comfort. I will give a few examples.

Micah 6 and 7 emotions in YHWH

6:3	How did I weary you?	*lā'āh*	past
6:7	Will YHWH be pleased with thousands of rams, with ten-thousand streams of oil?	*rāṣāh*	
7:7	I will await the God of my salvation		future
7:9	I will bear the rage of YHWH	*zaʻap yhwh*	future

Especially, in the final sub-canto of chapter 7, the emotive language on God is very strong:

Final sub-canto

7:18	Who is a god like you who forgives iniquity who passes by the transgression of the remnant of his inheritance? Who does not make firm his **anger** forever, because he has a **delight** in kindness.
7:19	He will turn, he will have **compassion** over us. He will subdue our iniquities. He will cast away into the depths of the sea all our sins.
7:20	You will give **fidelity** to Jacob, **loving-kindness** to Abraham as you swore to our ancestors in distant days

Five Hebrew words referring to emotions are used in this unit: *'ap*, 'anger'; *ḥāpēṣ*, 'delight'; *rāḥam* Pi., 'to have compassion'; *'èmèt*, 'fidelity; faithfulness'; *ḥèsèd*, 'loving kindness'. These five virtues (or attributes) give testimony of the caring side in God. The incomparability of God is seen in his ability to turn anger into compassion. This divine virtue steers and guides the divine acts: the forthcoming salvation of Israel. The absence of this kind of emotional motivational language in Micha 1–5 should be construed as a literary critical or redaction historical argument for the separation of the sections.

Micah 5:14 might be a caveat:

> 5:14 I will take vengeance in anger and fury
> on the people who did not listen.

This verse made me wobble for a while. It gnawed at my certainty. It seemed to undermine my point. I even thought to surrender and cancel this presentation. There is, however, a solution for every problem. 5:14 is at the very end of Micah 1–5. I would propose to construe 5:14 as a redactional hinge to connect 1:1–5:13 with 6–7. In doing so, I can uphold my view and do not feel urged to 'commit it to the flames'.[13]

5 Conclusion

The analysis above makes clear that the view of Cruz concerning the literary unity of the Book of Micah cannot be substantiated by the use of metaphors by the authors of that prophetic book. My observations have added an extra argument for the literary-critical separation of Micah 6–7 from the rest of this prophetic book.

---

13 See on this famous dictum Hume, "Commit It to the Flames".

That is Really Good: Remarks on Micah 6,8

1 Introduction

How to lead a morally decent life?[1] Despite the tendency to individualization in modern culture[2] and the loss of the great narratives,[3] many people want to live a morally decent life. For an answer to the question: what is morally decent, there is nowadays a great lack of examples or guidelines. The end of the great narratives and the melt-down of traditional ideologies (of whatever character) not only liberated people from sultry, prescriptive morality, but also made us stand ethically naked in front of the greater questions of life.[4] Some want to fill that void with a return to the narrow-mindedness of the post WW II era. I think that Francis Landy will agree with me that such a move is not preferable since it would deprive us of our personal responsibilities. I therefore propose to have a look at an open-minded text from the Hebrew tradition:

> He has told you, O man, what is good;
>> and what does the Lord require of you
> but to do justice, and to love kindness,
>> and to walk humbly with your God?[5]

2 Micah 6–7: A Josianic Reapplication

In the final chapters of the Book of Micah a different voice can be heard. This voice differs from the harsh language of unavoidable destruction in Micah 1 as well as from the interplay between salvation and doom in Micah 2–5. Over forty years ago Van der Woude proposed a literary-critical division between (1)2–5 and 6–7.[6] In my opinion this distinction is still valid[7] but I do not share Van der

---

1 It is with great pleasure that I offer my thoughts on this ancient text to Francis Landy. Once, while driving together through the Canadian Rockies, he asked me: what is it that you do (in scholarship)? I hope Francis will find an answer in this essay. Besides, since the secondary literature on the Book of Micah equals a tsunami, I had to make a choice.

2 See, e.g., Bauman, *Society Under Siege*.

3 See Lyotard, *Condition postmoderne*.

4 See, e.g., Bauman, *Does Ethics Have a Chance*.

5 Micah 6,8; ESV; my own translation follows later.

6 Van der Woude, "Deutero-Micha"; he applied this view in his Dutch language commentary Van der Woude, *Micha*, 195–99. In fact, Van der Woude is reviving an old exegetical tradition, see e.g. Burkitt, "Micah 6 and 7"; Eissfeldt, "Psalm aus Nord-Israel"; Willis, "Reapplied Prophetic Hope Oracle".

7 Despite other positions, such as Ben Zvi, *Micah*; O'Brien, *Micah* (who construe the Book of Micah as a text written in the Persian period); and Mays, *Micah*, 29–33; Wolff, *Dodekapropheton 4*;

https://doi.org/10.1515/9783111208657-011

Woude's conclusion that Deutero-Micah should be depicted as a prophet from Northern Israel living about a decade before the fall of Samaria. I propose to read this pseudepigraphic text against a different historical background, namely that of the time of King Josiah in the second half of the seventh century BCE. The text joins in the chorus of hope for the restoration of the Davidic dream of unity and for the return of the exiled Samarians. An interesting question would be, why were these chapters added to the book of Micah in those days? My intuition would be that in circles of the Jahweh-Allein Bewegung the prophet Micah was claimed to be one of the important ancestors of the movement.[8] The addition of the two pseudepigraphic chapters can then be seen as an appropriation to the period of transition from 'Manasseh' to 'Josiah'.

3 Micah 6,1–8: Text and Translation

Let me start with my translation of these six verses:

1   Hear now what YHWH is saying:
    'Stand up, plead before the mountains
      and let the hills hear your voice!'
2   Hear, o mountains, the plead of YHWH
      and the perennial foundations of the earth,
    since there is a strife[9] for YHWH
      with his people
        and with Israel he will dispute.
3   'My people, what have I brought on you?[10]
      and how did I weary you?
    Answer me!

Kessler, *Micha*, esp. 255–56; Cuffey, *Literary coherence*, esp. 313–14; Corzillius, *Michas Rätsel*, esp. 385–425 (who see the Book of Micah as the end result of a complex redaction history that lasted into the Persian period). His position is contested by all those scholars who operate within the theory that the present book of the 12 minor prophets is the final result of a very complex redaction-historical process in which the texts of the various prophetic traditions influenced each other; on this Dodekapropheton-theory see, e.g., Nogalski, *Literary Precursors*; Wöhrle, *Frühen Sammlungen*; Wöhrle, *Abschluss des Zwölfprophetenbuches*; Albertz, Nogalski, Wöhrle (eds), *Perspectives*; interesting remarks on this approach can be found in Roth, *Israel und die Völker*, 172–232. Van der Woude's position is adopted by Strydom, "Micah of Samaria"; Joosten, "YHWH's Farewell".

8 See Lang, "Jahwe-allein-Bewegung".

9 Note that the meaning of the word *rîb* has slightly shifted between verse 1 and 2; on the semantics as well as the legal connotations of *rîb* see: Harvey, *Plaidoyer prophétique*; Nielsen, *YAHWEH as Prosecutor*; Jensen, *Ethical Dimensions*, 133–34.

10 The construction of the verb *'aśah* with the preposition *le* should be construed as expressing the concept 'to bring something (bad) over someone else'.

4   For I have brought you up from the land of Egypt,
     I have ransomed you out of the house of slaves.
  I have send before you Moses, Aaron, and Miriam.
5   My people, remember
  What Balaq, the king of Moab, advised
     and what Balaam, the son of Beor, answered him.
  From Shittim to Gilgal
     in order to know the righteous acts of YHWH'.
6   'Wherewith shall I approach YHWH
     and prostrate myself before God on high?
  Shall I approach him with burnt offerings,
     With one year old calves?
7   Will YHWH be pleased with thousands of rams,
     with ten-thousand streams of oil?
  Shall I give my first-born for my transgression,
     the fruit of my womb for my personal sin?'
8   'He has told you, human, what is good
     and what YHWH requires of you:
  to do justice, to love kindness,
     and to act deliberately by walking with your God.'

Micah 6,1–8 is an intriguing text in which the appropriation of the Micah-traditions to the period of king Josiah is easily detected. In the form of a judicial ordeal, the unit adapts various themes from Micah 2–5. Although the unit does only contain two words from the semantic field of trespassing, the idea as such is clearly implied. YHWH presents himself as the God who had guided the people of Israel through its darkest hours in history mirroring the implied divine conduct in the oracles of salvation in Micah 2–5. Micah 6, however, displays a different view on morality. While Micah 2–5 refers to a whole set of specific transgressions, and hence can be construed as written in the dimensions of a casuistic code, Micah 6,8 offers a basic rule that should be taken as the foundation of human conduct. Historically, this shift in moral orientation coincides with the reformation in the times of Josiah.[11] I construe this reformation not only as a form of political power play on behalf of the newly formed priestly elite in Jerusalem, but also as an incentive to reframe the role of the cult in connection with appeasing the divine.

---

11 The historicity of the account in 2 Kings 22–23 is heavily debated; see, e.g., Lemche, "Did a Reform like Josiah's Happen?"; Monroe, *Josiah's Reform*; Na'aman, "Discovered Book"; Albertz, "Deuteronomistic History"; Blenkinsopp, "Remembering Josiah". I have no space here to defend my somewhat obsolete view that at least some changes in the religious life of Ancient Israel took place some fifty years before the Babylonian Exile.

4 The Composition of Micah 6

The Masoretic text in the Codex Leningradensis delimits Micah 6 with a *setumah* before verse 1, a *setumah* after verse 8, and a *petucha* after verse 16. These markers indicate that the Masoretes construed Micah 6 as containing two sub-cantos: 1–8 and 9–16. A thorough study of the layout-markers in Hebrew, Greek, Syriac, and Latin manuscripts in combination with an analysis of the poetic devices in this chapter, lead Johannes de Moor to the following proposal of the composition of Micah 6:[12]

Micah 6	Sub Canto	Canticle	Strophe	
	A: 1–8	A.i: 1–2	A.i.1:	1
			A.i.2:	2
		A.ii: 3–5	A.ii.1:	3
			A.ii.2:	4
			A.ii.3:	5
		A.iii: 6–8	A.iii.1:	6
			A.iii.2:	7
			A.iii.3:	8
	B: 9–16	B.i: 9–13	B.i.1:	9
			B.i.2:	10–11
			B.i.3:	12–13
		B.ii: 14–16	B.ii.1:	14
			B.ii.2:	15
			B.ii.3:	16

Fig. 1: The Structure of Micah 6 according to J. C. de Moor.

This proposal yields two questions. (1) Does the division into three canticles of sub-canto A tally with the contents of these lines? (2) Is this analysis strong enough to argue for the view that Micah 6 is to be construed as one coherent whole and not to be separated into two or three independent textual units as the mainstream of scholarship assumes?[13]

5 The Contents of Micah 6,1–8

Does the division into three canticles of Micah 6,1–8 make sense? In my view it does. Micah 6,1–2 contains a summons by YHWH to his people (*'ammô*) taking the

---

12 See De Moor, "Micah 6".
13 See De Moor, "Micah 6", esp. 90–95.

invariably permanent elements of creation as a witness in a law-suit against his permanently variable people. The mountains on the earth and the foundations below are summoned to continue their trustworthy part on the scene of history.

Micah 6,3–5 presents a summary of the past. This textual unit resembles the deuteronomistic view on the history of Israel with its dual emphasis on the goodness of God and the trespasses of 'his people'. To apply a phrase coined by Ehud ben Zvi: 'God has been a good patron',[14] while Israel did not meet the divine expectations and their own promises. Gods patronage is apparent in his defence plea in vss. 5–6. This historical retrospect thus refers to three important traditions. (1) The Exodus out of Egypt; (2) The inimical threat during the journey through the dessert,[15] and (3) The conquest of the Holy Land.[16]

Micah 6,7–8 can be construed as referring to the reaction of 'his people'. The divine plea apparently evoked a consciousness of having failed among the people of Israel. They seek to appease the divine with excessive and almost impossible gifts: thousands of rams and even the life of the firstborn child. This merchandising proposal, however, is countered with an instruction by an unmarked voice that is much more human and humane:

> to do justice,
> > to love kindness,
> > > and to walk perceptively with your God.[17]

In sum, the division into three canticles of Micah 6,1–8 tallies with the contents of these units.[18]

Canticle	Strophe
A.i: 1–2	Summons to a law-suit
A.ii: 3–5	Historical retrospect
A.iii: 6–8	Morality instead of abundant offerings

Fig. 2: Connections between canticle and content in Micha 6,1–8.

---

14 Ben Zvi, *Micah*, 145.

15 See Num. 22–24; see L. Schmidt, "Bileamüberlieferung".

16 Shittim was the last stopping place before the crossing of the Jordan (Josh. 3,1); Gilgal the first dwelling place in the promised land (Josh. 4,19). See, e.g. Van der Woude, *Micha*, 213; Andersen, Freedman, *Micah*, 523; Burnett, "Going Down".

17 Mic. 6,8; see T. F. Torrance, "Famous Saying"; Barstad, *Religious Polemics*, 113–14; Hillers, *Micah*, 75–79; Werner, "Micha **6:8**"; Andersen, Freedman, *Micah*, 525–30; Carroll, "He Has Told You"; Kessler, *Micha*, 256–72; Dreisbach, "Micah 6: 8"; De Moor, "Micah 6", 78–113; Hyman, "Questions and response"; Jeremias, *Propheten*, 197–205; Decorzant, *Vom Gericht zum Erbarmen*.

18 See also Ben Zvi, *Micah*, 141–42 (who however construes verse 6 to be a separate unit); Jacobs, *Conceptual Coherende*, 156–83; Waltke, *Micah*, 366–67; O'Brien, *Micah*, 73–93.

6 Is Micah 6 a Coherent Whole?

A vast majority of scholars divide Micah 6 into two or more parts and treat these sections as separate units.

Mays[19]	1–5	6–8	9–16
McKane[20]	1–5	6–8	9–16
Van der Woude[21]	1–8		9–16
Wolff[22]	1–8		9–16
Hillers[23]	1–8		9–16
Kessler[24]	1–8		9–16
Andersen, Freedman[25]	1–8		9–16
Ben Zvi[26]	1–8		9–16
Jacobs[27]	1–8		9–16
Jeremias[28]	1–8		9–16
Waltke[29]	1–8		9–16

Fig. 3: Division of Micah 6 by various scholars.

De Moor's analysis of the structure of Micah 6 gives rise to the idea that this chapter could be seen as a coherent whole.[30] There is, however, a minor problem with this view. As De Moor observed Micha 6,3–8 and 9–16 show an identical macrostructure of two canticles with three strophes each. This yields the question on the compositional position of Micah 6,1–2. I would like to argue that Micha 6,1–2 should be treated as a separate sub-canto introducing a twofold litigation (*rîb*) in 3–8 and 9–16:

---

19 Mays, *Micah*, 127–49.
20 McKane, *Micah*, 177–206.
21 Van der Woude, *Micha*, 200–39.
22 Wolff, *Micha*, 136–73.
23 Hillers, *Micah*, 75–82.
24 Kessler, *Micha*, 256–83.
25 Andersen, Freedman, *Micah*, 500–60.
26 Ben Zvi, *Micah*, 141–65.
27 Jacobs, *Conceptual Coherence*.
28 Jeremias, *Die Propheten*, 196–218.
29 Waltke, *Micah*, 342–415.
30 De Moor, "Micah 6", esp. 90–95.

Micah 6	Sub Canto
	A: 1–2
	B: 3–8
	C: 9–16

Fig. 4: The Structure of Micah 6 according to B. Becking.

This suggestion tallies with a recent proposal by Julia O'Brien. In her view '… the entirety of Mic 6 constitutes an imaged legal dispute … in which God is both accuser and judge'.[31] The dispute then contains two rounds of argument. In the first round (3–8) Israel is addressed as 'his people'. In the second round more specific addresses are found: *'îr*, 'city' (9), and *maṭṭēh*, 'tribe' (9). In the final strophe, two kings are named for their wicked deeds: *'āmrî*, 'Omri', and *'aḥāb*, 'Ahab' (16). In the first round the divine patronage is specified in the historical retrospect. In the second round, the trespasses of the people are specified by a set of words from the language of guilt, such as: *rāšā'*, 'wickedness' (10–11), *ḥāmās*, 'violence' (12), *šèqèr*, 'lie' (12), *rᵉmiyyāh*, 'deceit' (12), *ḥāṭᵉ'āh*, 'sin' (13). The first round ends with the famous saying on moral conduct which is presented as a possible way out of doom and misery. The second round ends with a clear prophecy of doom containing a strophe resembling the futility-clauses as found in the curses in various Neo-Assyrian texts:

> You will eat,
> > but you will not be satisfied,
> And your vileness will be in your midst.
> You will try to remove for safekeeping,
> > But you will not preserve anything,
> And what you do preserve
> > I will give to the sword.
> You will sow but
> > you will not reap.
> You will tread the olive but
> > will not anoint yourself with oil;
> And the grapes,
> > but you will not drink wine.[32]

---

31 O'Brien, *Micah*, 74; see already Willis, "Reapplied Prophetic Hope Oracle"; Sweeney, *Twelve Prophets*, 346, 393–405.
32 Micah 6, 14–15; see Becking, "Micah in Neo-Assyrian Light".

It is remarkable to see that in both sections the verb *hālak*, 'to go; walk', occurs in the final strophe:

B.ii.3 (8)   'to walk with your God'.
C.ii.3 (16)   'you walked in their counsels'.

There is a clear opposition between these two clauses.[33] In verse 8 the moral conduct of 'my people' is summoned to be anchored in the divine patronage, while in verse 16 it is stressed that in the past 'my people' followed the instructions of the 'statutes of Omri ... and Ahab'. This implies that the people is rebuked for putting their faith and trust in what is seen as human religious regulations allegedly derived from 'other gods' whose images were erected by these kings.

These observations and their interpretations lead me to the conclusion that the conceptual coherence of Micah 6 can be formulated in parallel with de Deuteronomic choice as formulated in Deut. 30:

See, I have set before you today life and good, death and evil. If you obey the commandments of YHWH, your God, that I command you today, by loving YHWH, your God, by walking in his ways, and by keeping his commandments and his statutes and his rules, then you shall live and multiply, and YHWH, your God, will bless you in the land that you are entering to take possession of it.[34]

In Deuteronomy Israel is triggered to make a choice between 'life' and 'death'. The *rîb* of YHWH with 'his people' results in a comparable choice between blessing and curse.

7 The Saying in Micah 6,8

It is important to note the following intertextual connection between Deut. 30,16 and Micah 6,8. Two of the four verbs occurring in Micah 6,8 are also attested in Deut. 30,16. The third verb *'āśāh*, 'to do', has a parallel in the verb *šāmar*, 'to keep'. The verb *ṣāna'* Hi., 'to behave prudently', has no parallel in Deut. 30,16. The verb is a hapax in the Hebrew Bible.

---

33 This opposition can be seen as an appropriation of a comparable statement in Micah 4,5. After the visionary display of the peaceful future, a conclusion at the level of human conduct is made: 'For all the peoples walk each in the name of its god, but we will walk in the name of YHWH, our God forever and ever'.
34 Deut. 30,15–16.

Verb	Deut. 30	object	Micah 6	object
'āśāh // šāmar	to keep	His commandments	to do	justice
'āhab	to love	Yʜᴡʜ, your God	to love	loyalty
ṣānaʿ	–	–	to behave modestly	–
hālak	to walk	in his ways	to walk	with your God

Fig. 5: Intertextual relations between Deut. 30,16 and Micah 6,8.

These relations underscore my assumption that it has been the function of Micah 6,8 to show 'his people' a way by which to avoid doom and curse. What is, however, the outline of this road?

A quick look at the renditions of this verse, ancient and modern, Bible translations and commentaries, shows a great variety. From the variation in these translations, it becomes clear that a few syntactical and linguistic problems exist in the interpretation of Micah 6,8 which now will be discussed.

Can the verse ben construed as containing a question? The first line of 6,8 clearly contains two clauses that could be read as questions: *māh-ṭôb*, 'what is good?', and *māh-yhwh dôrēš mimmᵉkā*, 'what does Yʜᴡʜ ask from you?'. These two clauses, however, are subordinated as accusative clauses to the main clause in the beginning of 6,8: 'He has told you'. Hence, they should not be construed as interrogative clauses. *māh* in the two clauses should not be rendered as interrogative pronouns[35] but should be considered as relative indicators.[36] This implies that the two last lines in 6,8 do not continue an interrogative clause and hence should not be translated as such.

Is there an antithesis between 6,8a an 8b? Some translations seem to opt for this position by putting a word like 'but' or 'other than' at the beginning of 8b. The Hebrew conjunction *kî* has a variety of meanings and can be applied syntactically in various ways.[37] In Micah 6,8 *kî* should be construed as an emphatic particle having explicative force. In my view, the clauses in 6,8b give an explanation of what is good.

How to construe the verb-forms? Micah 6,8b contains four verb-forms that all are infinitives. This implies that a translation with finite verb-forms is to be rejected as an interpretative paraphrase.

Is there a 'Wort Gottes'-theology in 6,8? Luther translated the noun *mišpāṭ*, 'justice', with 'Gottes Wort'. Although the regulations of are spelled out in the

---

35 Thus, e.g., Andersen, Freedman, *Micah*, 503.
36 Waltke, O'Connor, *Biblical Hebrew Syntax*, § 18,2–3.
37 See, e.g., Schoors, "Particle כִּי"; Clines, *DCH* IV, 383–91; Meyer, "Particle כִּי".

Hebrew Bible, especially in the Pentateuch or Torah – which have often been construed as the Word of God – there are no traces of the concept of a 'Wort Gottes'-theology in 6,8.

Is *haṣnēaʿ* an adverb? A vast majority of translations as well as scholars render this verb-form with an adverbial accusative of state: 'humbly'.[38] An interesting exception is the rendition in the LXX: καὶ ἕτοιμον εἶναι τοῦ πορεύεσθαι μετὰ κυρίου θεοῦ σου. The majority view seems to have a ground in grammar: the infinitive absolute can function as an adverb.[39] It is to be remarked, however, that *haṣnēaʿ* is an infinitive construct. The infinitive absolute in this clause is *lèkèt*. In their section on the adverbial use of infinitives, Waltke and O'Connor seem to blur the categories of infinitive construct and absolute by rendering *haṣnēaʿ* with an adverb and the infinitive absolute *lèkèt* with an infinitive. Since the verb-form *haṣnēaʿ* is followed by an infinitive, it would be more sound to translate 'and to behave prudently by walking ...'. As for the meaning of the root *ṣnʿ* Van der Woude correctly noted that the word should be construed as a wisdom-term.[40] The root is also attested in texts like Prov. 11,2; Sirach 16,25; 35,3. Hence, a translation with 'to act prudently, deliberately' should be preferred over the traditional rendition 'to act humbly'.[41]

All these remarks an considerations lead me to the following translation of Micah 6,8:

> He has told you, human, what is good
>> and what YHWH requires of you:
> to do justice, to love kindness,
>> and to act deliberately by walking with your God.

8 Back to Our Times

What exactly does that mean? Phrased this way, that is the wrong question. Because it is asking for readymade answers, while a basic attitude is referred to in

---

38 See also: Mays, *Micah*, 142; McKane, *Micah*, 192; Kessler, *Micha*, 271; Sweeney, *Twelve Prophets*, 400; Andersen, Freedman, *Micah*, 503; Jacobs, *Conceptual Coherence*, 183; Jensen, *Ethical dimensions*, 134; Joosten, 'YHWH's Farewell', 450; O'Brien, *Micah*, 88.
39 See Gesenius, Kautzsch, Cowley, *Hebrew Grammar*, § 113.2; Wolff, *Micha*, 138; Waltke, O'Connor, *Biblical Hebrew Syntax*, § 35,3,3b.
40 Van der Woude, *Micha*, 219; elaborating on an idea of Hyatt, "Micah 6:8".
41 Van der Woude, *Micha*, 219; adopted by Wolff, *Micha*, 17 'aufmerksam'; Waltke, *Micah*, 343, 394: 'wisely'; Hillers, *Micah*, 75–76; Runions, *Changing Subjects*, 168; pace, e.g., Clines, *DCH* VII, 136–37.

the words of Micah and not the guidelines for a casuistic morality. Many people tend to think immediately of rules and regulations about what is possible and what is not and which is the best behavior. Micah grasps beyond all that by stating three basic attitudes as the beams of morality. I interpret Micah's position as an example of what Max Weber would call 'ethics of disposition': a human being is personally responsible for his/her deeds and doings.[42] The contents of 'doing right' refer to an attitude that takes into account the codes of God and that does justice to other humans.[43] What matters is the love of solidarity and community spirit. We are not invited to be like a loose particle going its own lonely way through the universe, but to realize that we are organically part of a larger whole and that we have our responsibilities for that larger whole. Not humility but an open eye for the Gebot der Stunde[44] would help the world to be a better place.

42 Weber, *Politik als Beruf.*
43 See, e.g., Wolff, *Micha,* 156–58; Kessler, *Micha,* 271–72; Hyman, "Questions and response"; Mostovicz, Kakabadse, "He has told you"; Becking, *Dwarse dromer,* 32–38; Dietrich, "Einübung".
44 This classical rule form ethics has gained a new deepening through the works of Dietrich Bonhoeffer; see Bonhoeffer, *Ethik*; with Feil, *Theologie Dietrich Bonhoeffers*; Tietz, *Dietrich Bonhoeffer.*

Gender Ambiguity in Micah 7:8–13 as a Reflection of Divine Gender

Notes on Micah 7:8–13

1 Introduction and Focal Questions

Were all prophets in Ancient Israel male? Might some have been female? Could some have had a gender-ambiguity? In addition to that: in what way does the gender of a prophet reflect the gender of the deity whose spokesperson the prophet is? I will start with a few remarks on the prophets mentioned in the Hebrew Bible and slowly move on to the provoking question on divine gender.

Since the vast majority of the prophets in the Hebrew Bible have a male gender, the phenomenon of Ancient Israelite prophecy has traditionally been construed as acted out by men.[1] Thanks to the movement of looking for female voices,[2] there now is more attention to the important role of women in Ancient Israelite prophecy and divination.[3] Prophets like Miriam, Deborah, Hulda, and many others now have a firm place in textbooks.[4] In this contribution, in view of the third question mentioned above, I would like to pay attention – not to yet another female prophet or diviner – but to an intriguing aspect of the prophet presented in the Book of Micah. Throughout the Book of Micah, this prophet is presented as a male character. In the superscription, for instance, Micah is introduced as a male person:

---

1 Still in Petersen, *Prophetic literature*, 5–14; Clines, "He-Prophets".

2 Starting with Pardes, *Countertraditions*; Brenner and Van Dijk-Hemmes, *On Gendering Texts*; Meyers, Craven, and Kraemer, *Women in Scripture*; Fuchs, *Sexual Politics*; Klein, *Deborah to Esther*, and see the essays in Claassens and Fischer, *Prophecy and Gender*.

3 See for instance Ackerman, "Mirjam", 47–80; Hamori, *Women's Divination*; Ackerman, *Women*, 252–80.

4 See for instance Blenkinsopp, *History of Prophecy*, 48–55; Gafney, *Daughters of Miriam*; Stökl, *Prophecy*; Maier, "Feminist Interpretation", 467–74; Nissinen, *Ancient Prophecy*; Nissinen, "Agency of Female Prophets", 161–84; Grey., "Female Prophetic Traditions".

Note: I would like to thank Anne-Marie Korte, Utrecht University, for her critical and stimulating remarks on a previous draft of this article. Especially, her remarks on 'gender-ambiguity' were very helpful.

https://doi.org/10.1515/9783111208657-012

> The word of Yhwh
>> came to Micah, the Morashtite,
>>> in the days of Jotham, Ahaz, Hezekiah, kings of Judah,
>> that he envisioned[5]
>>> with regard to Samaria and Jerusalem. (Micah 1,1)

Here, the redactor of the final composition construes Micah with a third person masculine form: ḥāzāh, 'he envisioned'. At some instances, Micah is described with first person pronominal forms which in Ancient Hebrew are gender neutral. For instance:

> Because of this, I will mourn
>> and howl,
> and go barefoot
>> and naked,
> I will make a wailing like the jackals
>> and mourning like the daughters of an ostrich. (Micah 1,8)

Against this background, the phrasing of an oracle in Micah 7 is surprising as will become clear.

2 Micah 7,8–13, introduction, translation, and a few remarks

The unit Micah 7:8–13 is part of the greater unit Micah 6–7. I construe these two chapters as a propagandistic treatise dating from the period before the reform of Josiah. In the final two chapters of the Book of Micah, a voice can be heard that differs from the one in the first five chapters. In my opinion, a clear breach of discourse between chapters 5 and 6 is observable. This shift is discernible in various ways:
- At the level of unit-delimitation. Markers in ancient manuscripts indicate that a new section has begun.[6]
- At the level of the literary forms or *Gattungen*. The lawsuit or admonition followed by a didactic reflection on the past and a dialogue on morality cannot be seen as the expected continuation of the oracles of doom and salvation in Micah 2–5.

---

5 Hebrew: ḥāzāh, third person masculine singular.
6 De Moor, "Micah 6"; De Moor, *Micah*, 277–80.

– At the level of phraseology. Van der Woude has listed seven features in the dimension of words and phrases in chapters 6–7 that do not match the language in chapters 2–5.[7]
– At the level of the description of God. Micah 6–7 contains language and metaphors that present Yʜᴡʜ as a divine being with a variety of emotions varying between anger and comfort, an element that is absent in chapters 2–5.
– At the level of social criticism. In Micah 6–7, the critique of the ruling elite is confined to the elements of bribery and manipulating weights and measures.

I therefore disagree with two groups of scholars: (1) Those who construe the Book of Micah as a coherent whole and hence, do not separate chapters 6–7 from 2–5, and (2) Those who construe the final form of the Book of Micah as the result of a complex process of redactional activity.

The unit Micah 7:8–13 contains two elements:
(1) an expression of confidence (7:8–10) and
(2) an oracle of doom for the enemy (7:11–13).

This second element, 7:11–13, is not to be construed as an oracle of salvation,[8] but as an oracle of doom for the grammatically feminine enemy; the oracle of salvation follows in vv. 14–17. By implication, 7:11–13 does not function as a motivation for the confidence uttered in vv. 8–10.

The historical location of the unit is disputed. Earlier scholars dated Micah 7,7–20 with not much argument to the Maccabean age.[9] On the basis of some connections with III Isaiah, many scholars have connected this section with the exilic/early-postexilic period, at a time when Jerusalem was conquered but the walls had not yet been rebuilt.[10] Van der Woude,[11] however, argued for a background of Micah 6–7 during the last years before the fall of Samaria. He bases this mainly on the mention of Carmel, Bashan, and Gilead as conquered territories (7:14), while Samaria was not yet sacked. Willis adopted the idea to separate literary-critically Micah 6–7 from the rest of the Book of Micah, but hinted at the following:
(1) there is a series of ambiguities in the unit making the identity of the enemy unclear;

---

7 Van der Woude, „Deutero Micha"; adopting Burkitt, "Micah 6 and 7"; accepted by Wagenaar, *Judgment and Salvation*, 49–54; Gruber, "Women's Voices", 2–3.
8 See Van der Woude, *Micha*, 253–58; contra Dempster, *Micah*, 18–81.
9 Still Nogalski, "Micah 7:8–20".
10 Nehemiah; see for instance Schütte, *Israels Exil in Juda*, 110–11.
11 Van der Woude (1971); Van der Woude (1976: 249).

(2) there are many intertextual links between Mic. 7,7–20 and ch. 10 of the Judaean prophet Isaiah, where the doom for the Northern Kingdom is presented as a warning for the leaders in Judah.[12]

Willis then proposes that the Micahian oracle was reapplied to a later Judaean situation: an original oracle was redacted in order to fit the new context. I would like to go one step further by assuming that there was no earlier text from the eighth century and that the author of Micah 6–7 composed this unit in the years preceding the reforms of Josiah while using the fate of Samaria as a warning sign.

The present text of the section is not in disorder and there are no features that would hint at the necessity to assume redactional layers. This leads to the following translation:

[8]Do not rejoice over me, my enemy.[a]
Although I have fallen,[b]
　　I will rise.[c]
Although I dwell in darkness,[d]
　　YHWH is my light!
[9]I will bear the rage of YHWH,[e]
　　since I have sinned against him,[f]
until He pursues my suit[g]
　　and executes justice for me.[h]
He will bring me out to the light.[i]
　　　I will look for his vindication.
[10]May my enemy see,[k]
　　May shame cover her[l]
who said to me:
　　"Where is YHWH your God?"[m]
My eyes will look down on her[n]
　　thereupon she will be a trampling place, like mud in the street.
[11]A day is coming when your walls will be strengthened.
　　That day the order of things will be far away.
[12]That day your attacker will come to you
　　to divide Assyria and the fortified cities,
To divide from rock to river;
　　from sea to sea;
　　　from mountain to mountain.
[13]The land shall become like a devastation
　　before the eyes of its inhabitants,
　　　for the fruits of their deeds.

---

12 Willis, "Reapplied Prophetic Hope Oracle".

A few remarks on the textual unit:

a. Throughout history, military victors are inclined to mock a conquered nation. The Neo-Assyrian kings gloated over their victories. Traces of this debasing custom are found in the Hebrew Bible; see for instance 2 Sam.1:20; Obad. 12; Ps. 35,19, 24; 38,17.

   The enemy has been identified with Edom;[13] Assyria;[14] a collective enemy;[15] or a personal enemy of the prophet.[16] Willis argues that it is part of the strength of the section that her identity cannot be unveiled.[17]

b. The author does not inform about this 'fall'. The context suggests a military collapse or the falling apart of the community.

c. In this clause the verb *qûm*, "to rise", does not refer to a resurrection after death, but hints at a recovery from a seemingly hopeless situation.[18]

d. The noun *ḥōšèk*, "darkness", is used here metaphorically. It hints at the perennial experience of total despair and misery, as in Book of Job and the Psalms. The "I"-character confesses that God is nevertheless like an *'ôr*, "light", bringing hope in dark times.

e. In this clause, the verb *nāśā'*, generally "to lift; to carry", has the connotation "to bear; suffer; endure".[19]

f. The "I"-character accepts that it was her transgressions that evoked God's anger. In this act of substitution and solidarity, the "I"-character takes on the transgressions of the leaders as depicted in the previous section.

g. In line with LXX – *dikayóoo*, "to justify; vindicate", the verb *rîb*, "to strive; conduct a lawsuit", should be construed as having a positive outcome for the "I"-character.

h. The noun *mišpāṭ*, "justice", refers in the Hebrew Bible to redemption, but sometimes to a verdict of guilty.

i. The Neo-Babylonian expression *ana nūri šūṣu*, "to liberate to the light", provides a nice parallel.[20]

j. The "I"-character is not so much looking at or indulging in the outcome of God's righteousness, but waiting for God's decision to happen.[21]

---

13 See Obad.; Psalm 137.
14 Van der Woude, *Micha*, 251–52); Nogalski, "Micah 7:8–20".
15 Smith, *Micah-Malachi*, 58; Hillers, *Micah*, 87.
16 De Bruin, "Reading the Book of Micah", 330.
17 Willis, "Reapplied Prophetic Hope Oracle".
18 See Van der Woude, *Micha*, 252.
19 See *DCH* V: 765.
20 BIN I 36:23; UET 4 184:15; see *CAD* A/2, 372; De Moor, *Micah*, 352.
21 Contra Van der Woude, *Micha*, 252–53.

k. With Andersen and Freedman,[22] I construe the verb form as a jussive express-
    ing the wish of the "I"-character – representing the whole of the community.
    The verb *rā'āh*, "to see", is not connected with an object here. Most probably
    the outcome of God's intervention is meant as object, but this interpretation
    is far from certain.

l. The noun *bûšāh*, "shame", refers to a painful feeling of humiliation or distress
    caused by the consciousness of one's wrong or foolish behavior.

m. This insulting question mocks both God and his people.

n. The verb *rā'āh*, "to see", is repeated, the direction of gaze, however, will be
    inverted as a result of God's intervention.

o. A *mirmās*, "trampling place", is mentioned a few times in the Hebrew Bible.
    For example, in the Song of the Vineyard, the fate of the disobedient vineyard
    is characterized through the language of reversal: it will be devastated
    and become a trampling-place (Isa. 5,5). In Mic. 7, a comparable reversal is
    present. The *ṭîṭ*, "clay", elsewhere a resource for building blocks, will in the
    future be reduced to *ṭîṭ*, "mud", as it covers streets. In sum, the once proud
    enemy will be turned into that which is worthless in her humiliation.[23]

3 General Interpretation of Micah 7,8–13

This very moving section connects with the depths of pain and joy, punishment
and salvation. A triangle is assumed: the "I"-character; a feminine enemy; and
the God of Israel. The internal relations are in a process of movement. As a
result of Israel's transgressions, God had punished them with the occupation by
a feminine enemy. Assyria, however, had overreached its hand by rejoicing over
the fate of Israel. The tides will turn again: Assyria will become prey to destruction and desolation. History, however, is never schematic. The relations between
nations are not as sober as the movements of pawns in a game of chess. The
changes between the players in the triangle just mentioned involve deeply felt
emotions: joy, awe, rage, love, solitude and destruction.

The "I"-character in this triangle plays a prophetic role. This character is said
to share the burden of the people of Israel which functions as divinely recognition
of the pain of the people. At the same time, this character is the service-hatch of
a message of hope.

---

22 Andersen and Freedman, *Micah*, 584.
23 See Waltke, *Micah*, 437.

4 The Gender of the Prophet

I now will return to the opening set of questions and apply them to the prophet in the Book of Micah. As noted above, the prophetic character is mainly seen as male. I would propose to see one instance in the Book of Micah where the prophet is construed as female. In Micah 7:10, the Hebrew text is intriguing, as the word *ᵉlōhāyik*, "your God", has a feminine suffix, implying that the prophetic "I" figure in this unit was construed as a woman, which would be unique in the Book of Micah. It should be noted that within the narrative communication this feminine presentation of the prophet is focalized by the author through the gaze of the enemy. At the syntactical level the presentation is found in the direct speech of the "enemy". It should be noted that elsewhere in the Hebrew Bible the suffix in *ᵉlōhāyik*, "your God", clearly refers to a female person.[24]

The fact that in 7:10 the prophet is presented as female, is sometimes explained by assuming the possibility that either someone other than Micah was envisioned – for instance the city of Jerusalem[25] or the collective inhabitants of Judah.[26]

The idea of a female prophet is challenged by De Moor. According to him, the speaking voices – or 'I'-characters in Mic. 7:1–6 and 7–10 must have been the same person.[27] Since it is obvious that the speaking voice in vv. 1–6 is a male person, the word *ᵉlōhāyik* in this verse is problematic in the perception of De Moor. Already in 1963, De Moor had published his observation that in two Hebrew manuscripts, the form *ᵉlōhēkā* is attested, with a masculine suffix.[28] Research in an abundance of Hebrew manuscripts made clear that about 35 % of these manuscripts read the form with a masculine suffix.[29] This argument seems impressive but is it convincing? First, the presence of a masculine suffix could also be interpreted as an exegetical adaptation in these manuscripts and hence is not an argument for an original masculine suffix. Second, when 35 % of the manuscripts show a masculine suffix, then 65 % of the manuscripts will have a feminine suffix which, in my opinion, is the majority and an argument for an original feminine suffix.

In my view, it would be better to accept the feminine suffix of the Masoretic text as the original form. The question then rises: how to interpret this observa-

---

24 Ruth 1,16 (Noomi); Isa. 51,22 (Jerusalem); 60,19 (Jerusalem).
25 Andersen and Freedman, *Micah*, 567; Ben Zvi, *Micah*, 168.
26 Runions, *Changing Subjects*, 177.
27 De Moor, *Micah*, 353–55.
28 De Moor, "Handschriften".
29 De Moor, "Micah 7: 1–13", 167; De Moor, *Micah*, 353–360. It should be noted that in a non-vocalized text the suffix in אלהיך could be both masculine and feminine.

tion? The presence of the feminine suffix is – to Gruber – an indication to construe Micah 6–7 as written by a female author.[30] This assumption is both unnecessary and uncontrollable.

In my view, the presence of the feminine suffix indicates something else. I interpret the phenomenon that 'Micah' or 'the prophet' was seen as a gender ambiguous human being. This person was neither male nor female and at the same time both feminine and masculine. If prophecy were to understand as the expression of an ecstatic mind or the phrasing of the experience of someone who had been in an otherworldly dimension, then in that state gender identity could become ambiguous or fluid.

5 A Neo-Assyrian Parallel

To support this view, I would like to have a look at prophets known from sources outside the Hebrew Bible. In the Neo-Assyrian archives some tablets were found that contained a collection of prophecies addressed to the kings Esarhaddon and Ashurbanipal. They were edited by Parpola[31] and have been extensively studied since then.[32] Almost all of the Neo-Assyrian prophets were related to the goddess Ishtar of Arbela. At times, they showed an 'odd behaviour' that should be construed as based on a process of identification with this goddess. As Martti Nissinen puts it: 'As proclaimers of the word of Ištar, the prophets acted *as* Ištar. The primary role of the prophets as intermediaries between the divine and the human spheres reflects the role of Ištar/Mulissu as the mediator between the gods and the king ...'.[33] In other words the final aim for all these 'prophets' would be a unification or identification with the goddess Ishtar.[34] So far, I have referred to Ishtar as a female deity, but basically she has an ambiguous gender identity in which the differences of the sexes are not stable.[35] Throughout the three millennia of religious devotion known to us from Sumer and Akkad, from Babylonia

---

30 Gruber, "Women's Voices".

31 Parpola, *Assyrian Prophecies*.

32 See e.g. Nissinen, *References to Prophecy*; Nissinen, "Socio-Religious Role"; Weippert, "König, fürchte dich nicht!"; De Jong, *Isaiah*, 171–88); Stökl, *Prophecy*; Stökl, "Gender Ambiguity"; Nissinen, *Ancient Prophecy*; May, "Women in Cult", 139–41.

33 Nissinen, "Socio-Religious Role", 96. In the Neo-Assyrian period, Mulissu was the name of the consort of the deity Assur. She is often identified with Ishtar.

34 Parpola, *Assyrian Prophecies*, xxxiv; See Frymer-Kensky, *Wake*, 30–31; Harris, "Inanna-Ishtar"; Colonna, "Archétype/Image archétypique"; Pryke, *Ishtar*, 60–83.

35 See Harris, "Inanna-Ishtar", 261–78); Frymer-Kensky, *Wake*, 58–69; Chapman, *Gendered Language*, 55–56; Esztári and Vér, "Voices of Ištar"; Pryke, *Ishtar*, 60–83.

and Assyria, Ishtar is related to concepts of shifts in gender roles. In an ancient Sumerian hymn to Inanna we read:

> May she (= Inanna/Ishtar) change the right side into the left side
>> Dress him in the dress of a woman
> Place the speech of a woman in his mouth
>> And give him a spindle and a hair-clasp.[36]

In the phrase 'to change the right side into the left side' the words 'right' and 'left' should be construed as euphemisms for 'male' and 'female'. The 'he' character in this strophe refers to a male cult functionary of Ishtar, a so-called *kurgarru* or *asinnu*.[37] Such functionaries were known as being dressed and as acting like women.[38] In a Hymn by Ashurbanipal to Ishtar of Nineveh it is said:

> O praised Emašmaš, ...[...], in which dwells Ištar, the que[en of Nineveh]!
> Like Aššur, she wears a beard and is clothed with brilliance [...]. The crown on her head g[leams] like the stars; the luminescent discs on her breasts shine like the sun![39]

The presentation of the female deity Ishtar with a manly beard – indicating 'her' gender ambiguity – is already present on an Old Babylonian cylinder seal.[40]

In the Neo-Assyrian prophetic texts, some documents hint at a quite fundamental personal shift. Some prophets seem to change their gender-role during the period of ecstasy. The Neo-Assyrian prophets and prophecies are known to us, since they were collected and archived on large tablets. These tablets contain sets of prophecies with the name of the prophet included. I would like to pay attention to two persons here: Bayâ and Illusa-amur. There is something strange with them. Bayâ occurs in the following oracle:

---

36 UM 29-16-229 ii 4f; see Sjöberg, "i n – n i n š à – g u r₄ – r a", 224); Helle, "Only in Dress?"; Steinert, "Ecstatic Experience"; Zgoll, "Innana and En-ḫedu-ana"; see also Erra Epic IV 56–58: "whose maleness Ishtar turned fe[male] for the awe of the people; carriers of swords, carriers of razors, scalpels, and blades, who break [taboos?] to Ishtar's delight!".
37 Helle, "Only in Dress?", correctly noted that the titles *kurgarru* and *asinnu* are among the Mesopotamian words denoting non-binary identities; see also May, "Women in Cult", 135.
38 See Stökl, *Prophecy*, 58–61.
39 *SAA* 3.7:4–8. See Esztári and Vér, "Voices of Ištar", 30.
40 The seal dates from the period around 1800 BCE and is now in The British Museum (BM130694); with Westenholz, "Inanna and Ishtar", 337; Esztári and Vér, "Voices of Ištar", 30.

ša pi-i ᴹⁱ.*ba-ia-a* DUMU ᵁᴿᵁ.*arba-ìl*
By the mouth of the woman Baya, son of Arbela[41]

The female determinative Mí before the personal name clearly hints at a female person. The name Bayâ is listed elsewhere as referring to women[42] as well as to men.[43] The Sumerogram DUMU, 'son', marks Bayâ as a male person coming from the city of Arbela.[44] Hence, Bayâ is of an unclear gender. With Illusa-amur – the name means 'I have seen her godhead', probably not a name given at birth – something comparable is at stake. Although the name is feminine, the grammatical construction indicating the place of birth, the gentilic adjective, refers clearly to a masculine person.[45] This indistinctness of the gender of these two prophets can be interpreted as a sign that they were 'men turned into women' and had an ambiguous gender. Some scholars offered the somewhat speculative view that this was the result of an act of self-castration.[46] The state of 'men turned into women' could better be interpreted as an indication that they reached their aim of being a genderfluid person, which makes them perfect for their role as mouthpiece of the goddess Ishtar.

I am not implying that all prophets from the ancient Near East were cast in an indistinct gender role. That view would easily be contradicted by the available evidence. I displayed the genderfluid persons Bayâ and Illusa-amur as illustration of the deeper motifs behind the frenzy or 'odd behaviour' of so many ecstatic persons and prophets from the Ancient Near East: the wish to be a pure and adequate vessel for the divine message by transcending into the likeness of the deity. I interpret the evidence as follows. Both Bayâ and Illusa-amur were seen as genderfluid human beings. In their role of prophet, they were neither male nor female and at the same time both feminine and masculine.[47]

---

41 SAA 9 1.4 ii:40'; see Parpola, *Assyrian Prophecies*, 6; see Nissinen e.a., *Prophets and Prophecy*, # 71 = 114–16, with lit.; the same line occurs in SAA 9 2.2 35'; see Nissinen e.a., *Prophets and Prophecy*, # 79 = 122–23, with lit.; Stökl, *Prophecy*, 122); Stökl, "Gender Ambiguity", 75–76; Esztári and Vér, "Voices of Ištar" 22–24

42 Parpola, *Assyrian Prophecies*, il.

43 Nissinen and Perroudon, "Bāia".

44 The argument of Weippert, "König, fürchte dich nicht!", 14.33; Stökl, "Gender Ambiguity", 75, that the Sumerogram DUMU is an abbreviated spelling for DUMU.MUNUS, *mārtu*, 'daughter', is not convincing.

45 See SAA 9 1.5, with see Parpola, *Assyrian Prophecies*, 6; see Nissinen e.a., *Prophets and Prophecy*, # 72 = 116, with lit., Stökl, *Prophecy*, 122–23); Stökl, "Gender Ambiguity", 73–75; Esztári and Vér, "Voices of Ištar", 22–24; May, "Women in Cult", 140.

46 Parpola, *Assyrian Prophecies*, il; see, however, the criticism in Weippert, "König, fürchte dich nicht!", 33.

47 See Stökl, "Gender Ambiguity"; Nissinen, *Ancient Prophecy*, 297–32.

6 The Prophet and the Deity in Micah 7,10

To what conclusions does this comparative detour lead? To me, it has shown that the gender ambiguity of the prophet in Micah 7 is not a unique phenomenon in the Ancient Near East. Besides, since the prophets were striving for one-ness with the divine and were seen as the likeness of the deity, a bold question emerges. Would it be possible to construe this gender ambiguity in Micah 7 as a sign for the idea that Yhwh, the God of Israel, in some cases was seen as having the same gender ambiguity? Does the gender-ambiguity of the prophet reflect a gender ambiguity in the Deity? Generally, Yhwh is construed as a male deity and many texts and images from the Hebrew Bible underscore this view.[48] Reading Micah 7 in the way I just did would imply that in certain circles of Ancient Israel and at certain times of its history, Yhwh was – comparable to the Mesopotamian god Ishtar[49] – seen as a divine being without a clear gender identity. Yhwh as a genderfluid deity was construed at times as neither male nor female and at the same time both feminine and masculine.

---

48 See two recent studies, one by a male: Lewis, *Origin and Character*, and one by a female scholar: Stavrakopoulou, *God*, who both argue for the masculinity of Yhwh.
49 See Frymer-Kensky, *Wake*; Parpola, *Assyrian Prophecies*, xxxiv; Harris, "Inanna-Ishtar"; Colonna, "Archétype/Image archétypique"; Pryke, *Ishtar*, 60–83.

Bien étonnés de se trouver ensemble

The Book of Micah and papyrus Amherst

1 Introduction

In this essay, I would like to make some comparisons between two texts from the ancient Near East that at first sight seem to be unconnected. The book of Micah, on the one hand, is a compendium of prophetic texts that can be seen as the final product of a tradition that started in Judah in the decades before 700 BCE and ended at an undeterminable time around the end of the Babylonian exile. The Aramaic Text in Demotic script known as Papyrus Amherst 63 too is a compendium of texts, although of an even broader variety.

That text has long been an enigma for scholars. The artefact was acquired by Lord Amherst of Hackney through an Egyptian agent as part of a collection of manuscripts in the final decade of the nineteenth century. Amherst was – like many of his peers – a collector of antiquities. Many Egyptian artefacts found their way to his private museum. After a financial debacle, the greater part of the collection had to be sold to a New York banker, through whom the set of papyri ended in the Pierpont Morgan library. A preliminary publication of papyrus Amherst 63[1] together with a set of photographs, stirred the minds of the Egyptologists. The text was written in clear Demotic signs, but they did not make sense. Obviously, the Demotic script was used to give words to a text in a different language. The then unsolved riddle was: which language? The key to the solution had been found in 1932 but the Semitist Noël Aimé-Giron who suggested that the language used probably was Aramaic.[2] In 1944, Raymond Bowman published a translation of four lines.[3] Thereafter the research went into a silent slumber. The work on papyrus Amherst 63 entered a faster gear after the discovery that a section of it formed a parallel with parts of the Biblical Psalm 20.[4] This lead to three editions of the text in its entirety.[5]

---

1 Newberry and Crum, *Amherst Papyri*.
2 In a letter to Herbert Thompsen dated August 7, 1932, see Van der Toorn, *Papyrus Amherst 63*, 3–4.
3 Bowman 1944.
4 pAmh 63 xii: 11–19; see Nims, Steiner, "Paganized Version"; Vleeming, Wesselius, "Aramaic Hymn".
5 Steiner and Nims, Aramaic Text in Demotic Script; Van der Toorn, *Papyrus Amherst 63*; Holm, *Aramaic Literary Texts*.

https://doi.org/10.1515/9783111208657-013

The text of papyrus Amherst 63 contains a collection of a variety of texts: hymns, dirges, prayers, love songs, and historical narratives. The coherence of all these sections is note prima facie clear. According to Van der Toorn, the text consists of five sections.[6] The first three sections can be connected to ethnic groups: Babylonians (col. i–v), Syrians (col. vi–xi), and Israelites (col. xii–xiii) and express their religious world views. The fourth section (col. xiv–xvii) is situated in the 'oasis in the desert'. This fourth section clearly witnesses the peaceful living together of the groups mentioned. The section has a clear syncretistic subtext. The final, fifth section (col. xviii–xxiii) is a kind of an appendix and contains the 'tale of two brothers', i.e. a narrative on the fate of the neo-Assyrian king Ashurbanipal and his rival brother Shamas-shumu-ukin.[7]

Although the text on the papyrus was written in the fourth century BCE, the contents reflect a much earlier period. It can be assumed that the text goes back to an Aramaic original from the seventh century.[8]

2 Prophetic Formula: An Imbalance

The text of Papyrus Amherst 63 contains – among many other genres – some passage of a prophetic character.[9] In the second section that focuses on the Syrians, on oracle of salvation is present:

a. Mar speaks up and says to me:
b. [...] my servant!
c. Fear not (אל תחדל)!
d. I will save you!
e. If you bow down for Mara, Mar from Darga and Rash.
f. [...].
g. in] your days
h. [your] e[nemies shall be] de[stroyed].
i. During your years
j. [your] fo[es] shall be slain.
k. [...] I
l. will destroy before you.
m. Your foot on their necks

---

6 For now, I adopt the delimitation by Van der Toorn, *Papyrus Amherst 63*, knowing that it is open to challenge and refinement.
7 First edition by Steiner and Nims, "Ashurbanipal".
8 See for instance Heckl, "Inside the Canon"; Van der Toorn, *Papyrus Amherst 63*.
9 See Becking, "Prophetic Elements".

n. [you will plant ...].
o. [I will support] your right hand
p. in all your land.
q. [You shall rule(?)] your house in peace.[10]

Almost at the end of the Syrian section of papAmh 63 a dream report is found:
a. In my dream I was young again,
b. I was transported to Rash.
c. I saw a city in Rash.
d. I went out and heard its name:
e. 'On-the-borders-of-Rash-she-is-founded'
f. Our Master protects 'On-the-borders'.
g. He will slay his trouble-maker on her fields.
h. He will smash with a righteous punishment.
i. His words will sustain me
j. Against his anger
k. So I shall be lifted
l. To the broad place of Mar.[11]

I will not enter here into a full discussion of these textual units and their function within the whole of the text of Papyrus Amherst 63.[12] I would like to concentrate on possible parallels with the book of Micah.

The oracle of salvation in Papyrus Amherst 63 contains the well-known formula: "Fear not (אל תחדל)!" These words – אל תחדל form the Aramaic equivalent of Akkadian *la tapallaḥ*, Ugaritic *al tdḥl*, and the Hebrew phrase אל תירא. The Aramaic expression is also attested in the inscription of king Zakkur of Hamath in the divine response to a royal prayer for diversion from sorrow.[13] This 'assurance of salvation' is present in a great number of prophetic passages in the Hebrew Bible – especially in Jeremiah and DeuteroIsaiah –. Astonishingly, it is absent in the book of Micah. The verb ירא, 'to fear', occurs only in Micah 6,9:

---

10 Pap Amherst 63 vii:12–17; see Van der Toorn, *Papyrus Amherst 63*, 120–24; for a different reading, see Steiner and Nims, "You Can't Offer Your Sacrifice"; Steiner and Nims, Aramaic Text in Demotic Script, 19–23; Nissinen e.a., *Prophets and Prophecy*, 10.
11 Pap Amherst 63 xi:8–13, see Steiner and Nims, Aramaic Text in Demotic Script, 37–39; Van der Toorn, *Papyrus Amherst 63*, 155–57.
12 As I already did in Becking, "Prophetic Elements".
13 *KAI* 202 A:13.

> The voice of Yhwh calls to the city.
> – It is prudence to fear[14] your name –.

This line, however, is not connected with the prophetic formula but should be read in the framework of wisdom-traditions in which 'to fear God' is an expression for deeply felt veneration.

The report in Papyrus Amherst 63 xi:8–13 narrates about a dream the unknown 'I'-figure had. This implies that a dream was understood as a medium for the gods to inform the humans.[15] In the Hebrew Bible, dreams are generally assessed as adequate communications of the divine will, as is clear from the narratives on Joseph and Daniel. A comparable positive assessment can be found in the Book of Numbers:

> When there are prophets among you,
> I, Yhwh, make myself known to them in visions;
> speak to them in dreams.[16]

Others texts, however, warn for dreams especially when the source of the dream is not clearly Yhwh.[17] In the Micah 3,5–8 a group of religious specialists especially those who give their message of peace in return to a piece of bread, is rebuked. Their punishment is described as follows: it will no longer be possible for them to contact the divine realm. God will be silent to them:

> It will be night for you, however, without vision
> and there will be darkness over you, without divination.
> The sun will go down over the prophets
> and the day will grow dark over them.
> The seers will be ashamed
> and the diviners confounded.[18]

---

14 The Masoretic vocalization *yir'èh*, 'he sees', is difficult to maintain. It leads to a bent clause containing incongruity between subject and verb: 'sound wisdom sees your name'. Since LXX (*foboúmenous*) and Vulg (timentibus) as well as the Targum and the Syriac translation have forms of the verb 'to fear', it is wise to assume a form of the verb *yārā'*, 'to fear', to be more original; see for instance Van der Woude *Micha*, 224; Andersen and Freedman, *Micah*, 539; Runions, *Changing subjects*, 169; De Moor, *Micah*, 296.

15 See, e.g., Cryer, *Divination*, 157–59.263–72; Jeffers, *Magic and Divination*, 125–43; Pongratz-Leisten, *Herrschaftswissen*, 96–127; Van der Toorn, *Scribal Culture*, 180–81; Noegel, *Nocturnal Ciphers*; Konstantopoulos, "Women and the Interpretation of Dreams".

16 Num. 12,6; see Jeffers, *Magic and Divination*, 128.

17 Deut. 13,1–5; Jer. 23,8, for instance.

18 See Korpel and De Moor, *Silent God*, 192–93; De Jong, "It Shall Be Night to You"; Boloje, "Trading Yahweh's Word".

It is remarkable, that in this list the concept of 'dream' is absent.

A third category to be discussed her is the woe-oracle. This term refers to a literary *Genre* in which a person or a group is bewailed beforehand. The background of the figure of speech is to be found in the mourning cry. After the death of a person, he or she is bewailed.[19] In applying this form to the still living, an author classifies the life of a person or a group as having entered a dead-end-street: a mourning cry will be their inevitable fate.[20] A woe-oracle traditionally is built up in three elements: address – accusation – announcement. The oracle in Micah 2 reads as follows:

Address	Woe to you who devise wickedness
	and who plan evil on their beds
Accusation	who execute it by the light of the morning,
	because it is in the power of their hands.
	When they desire fields,
	they rob,
	and houses,
	they take.
	They extort a fellow and his house,
	a man and his inherited yard.
Announcement	Therefore, thus says YHWH:
	"Behold, I will devise an evil against this clan
	out of which you cannot remove your neck.
	You shall not walk haughtily
	because this will be an evil time.
	On that day, one will recite a saying over you,
	there will be a bitter, wailing weeping
	namely:
	"We are completely destroyed.
	The portion of my people, he changed.
	How has he removed it from me!
	He has divided our fields among the rebellious!"
	You, however, will have no-one
	Who will cast by lot the measuring line
	in the community of YHWH."[21]

---

19 See Olyan, *Biblical Mourning*.
20 Westermann, *Grundformen*, 137–42; Janzen, *Mourning Cry*; Hillers, *Micah*, 31; Wagenaar, *Judgment and Salvation*, 208–20.
21 Mic. 2,1–5.

As far as I can see, the woe-oracle is infrequent in other ancient Near Eastern texts. A nice example is found in the *ade*-regulation – or treaty – between Aššur-nerari, king of Assyria, and Mati'-ilu, the ruler of Bît-Agusi:

> If Mati'-ilu sins against this treaty with Aššur-nerari, king of Assyria, may Mati'-ilu become a prostitute, his soldiers women, may they receive [a gift] in the square of their cities like any prostitute, may one country push them to the next; may Mati'-ilu's (sex) life be that of a mule, his wives extremely old; may Ištar, the goddess of men, the lady of women, take away their bow, bring them to shame, and make them bitterly weep: "Woe (*a-ḫu-la*), we have sinned against the treaty of Aššur-nerari, king of Assyria."[22]

In this text, the three elements – address – accusation – announcement – occur albeit in a different order. My hope that the text of Papyrus Amherst 63 would contain a woe-oracle turned out to be in vain.

I sum, there does not seem much that both texts have in common. Fortunately, there is one feature that both share.

3 The Incomparability of Yнwн

The Biblical Book of Micah ends with an eulogy on the caring incomparability of the God of Israel:

18 Who is a god like you
>   who forgives iniquity
>   who passes by the transgression of the remnant of his inheritance;
>   who does not make firm his anger forever,
>   because he has a delight in kindness?
19 He will turn, he will have compassion over us.
>   He will subdue our iniquities.
>   You will cast away into the depths of the sea
>   all their sins.
20 You will give fidelity to Jacob,
>   loving-kindness to Abraham
>   as you swore to our ancestors
>   in distant days.[23]

---

22 SAA 2, 2: r. 8–14.
23 Micah 7,18–20, own translation; for philological and exegetical remarks see my forthcoming commentary in the Anchor Yale Bible on Micah.

This hymn contains two elements, looking forward and backward. Verse 18 is a rhetorical question that plays with the name of the prophet.[24] Micah 7,19–20 depicts the impending deeds of liberation by God. In the meantime the text looks back at the memory of past acts of God that function as an argumentum ad Deum.[25] The hope that God will act in a way comparable to the past functions as a motivation to the prayer in Micah 7,14–17. The section is clearly an appropriation of the testimonial creed in Exod. 34,6–7 to the times of the author.[26]

In my opinion, the unit fits the period just before the reign of king Josiah in view of its hopes for redemption. De Moor argues for a slightly later date: the final days of the exile/early period after the return.[27] Jeremias assumes that 7:18–20 are to be construed as the latest redactional addition to Micah.[28] He argues that in the Maccabean age the reference to this old creed would be a seam through the whole of the Dodekapropheton Book. A comparable view is proposed by Wöhrle who construes 7:18–20 to be part of the final redactional layer of the Book of the Twelve, the 'Gnaden Korpus' (grace-redaction).[29]

In this short hymn, the author combines two theological concepts. The idea that Yʜwʜ is incomparable with any other deity, is connected with the traditional testimony on an interfering and caring God, as for instance phrased in Exodus 34. The hymn expresses hope. In applying the ancient creed to his own time, the author tries to persuade Yʜwʜ to act again on behalf of his people in need and misery. The everlasting solidarity of God is hoped to be the source of a new redemptive future.[30]

The rhetorical question "who is like you?" touches the theme of divine incomparability. Yʜwʜ's incomparability assumes (1) the acceptance of the existence of other deities and (2) a proclamation that these deities are not on a par with the God of Israel.[31] The incomparability of God is often underscored with references to the lack of supporting abilities of the other gods (see Jer. 10; DtIsa).[32] Mic.7 takes a different, positive lane by enumerating the virtues of Yʜwʜ.

---

24 The name of the prophet *mîkāh*, 'Micah', is generally seen as a shorter form of *mîkāyāh* or *mîkā'ēl*, 'who is like god'.
25 See Sanders, "Argumenta ad deum".
26 See for instance Brueggemann, *Theology*, 141–42; Jenson, *Obadiah, Jonah, Micah*, 187–89; Cruz, "Who is like Yahweh?", 223–26; Di Fransisco, "He Will Cast their Sins"; De Moor, *Micah*, 375–79; Lewis, *Origin and Character of God*, 569.
27 De Moor, *Micah*, 365–71.
28 Jeremias, *Propheten*, 222–23.
29 Wöhrle, *Abschluss*, 335–419; see also Scaiola, "Twelve".
30 See Smith, *Micah-Malachi*, 59; Brueggemann, *Theology*, 141–42; Waltke, *Micah*, 462–66.
31 Labuschagne, *Incomparability*; Kessler, *Micha*, 309; Banister, *God of Thunder and War*, 44–46.
32 Middlemas, *Divine image*, 93–102.

4 Comparable Passages in the Hebrew Bible

The rhetorical question "who is like you?" occurs a few times in the Hebrew Bible. I will mention some of the attestations. Their song after the passage through the Red Sea Moses and Miriam sing:

> Who among the gods
>   is like you, YHWH?
> Who is like you –
>   majestic in holiness,
> awesome in glory,
>   working wonders?[33]

In an individual lament, the Psalmist utters the following conviction:

> Among the gods there is none like you, YHWH;
>   no deeds can compare with yours.
> All the nations you have made
>   will come and worship before you, YHWH;
>   they will bring glory to your name.
> For you are great and do marvellous deeds;
>   you alone are God.[34]

Both texts accept the existence of gods other than YHWH. Both texts argue with his great and salvific deeds to contrast YHWH with the other gods.

5 Comparable Passages outside the Hebrew Bible

It would be expected in polytheistic religions that the notion of incomparability does not occur in them since all gods were venerated albeit for different aspect of life. Interestingly, many passage in extra-biblical texts contain the theme of incomparability.[35] In several hymns, epics, and incantations a variety of Mesopotamian, Egyptian, and Ugaritic deities is said to be. They are presented as surpassing the other deities who cannot be equalled with them. In a Mesopotamian text from the Kassite period the sun god Shamash is presented as without a real rival:

---

33 Ex. 15:11; Labuschagne, *Incomparability*, 16–28; Lewis, *Origin and Character of God*, 578–79.
34 Psalm 86:8–10.
35 A good collection still is Labuschagne, *Incomparability*, 31–63; see also Middlemas, *Divine image*, 102–04.

1. [...] deity, without [equal. ...],
2. [who holds] the [hea]ven in his hand
3. [the lord of the horn] and the hurdle(s),
4. [who gives an heir (?)] And a good name,
5. [who gives a rifle], the creator of man,
6. [at] the appearance of the Sin, the gods, who [kings
7. make their pure sacrifice, press their face (on the earth),
8. to colonize and devastate countries,
9. to make enemies, to let fight with one another,
10. one waits for the lamp, (for) Sin.
11. Except Sin and Šamaš
12. no other god answers "yes" in heaven.
13. Sin in heaven does not bind without Šamaš,
14. Sceptre, king's cap, throne, ruler's dress (?), Where (are they)?
15. To the king and his country
16. it would not exist without Šamaš.[36]

For the author of the hymn, Shamash was to be seen as an incomparable deity in view of the god's ability to reign heaven and earth.

In the Babylonia epic of creation, the god Marduk is lauded by the other deities:

> You are the great chief among the great gods,
>   you fate is unequalled, your command is Anu!
> O, Marduk, you are the great chief among the great gods,
>   your fate is unequalled, your command is Anu!
> Therefore, your command shall not be without avail,
>   In your power shall it be to exalt and to abase[37]

In this passage the incomparability of Marduk expresses his highest rank among the gods and his position of commander in chief over gods and creation.

In the great hymn to Aten – often seen as a parallel to Psalm 104[38] – the so-called monotheism of Echnaton is expressed, for instance with the following words:

---

36 *KAR* I 19:1–16; see Ebeling, "Hymnus"; Labuschagne, *Incomparability*, 35; Foster, *Before the Muses*, 747–78.
37 Enuma Elish IV:3–8; see Talon, *Enūma Eliš*, 15, 51, 91; Kämmerer, Metzler, *Weltschöpfungsepos*.
38 See Day, "Psalm 104".

> O sole god, like whom there is no other!
>> You created the world according to you desire,
> Whilst thou were alone: All men, cattle, and wild beasts,
>> Whatever is on Earth, going upon (its) feet,
>>> And what is on high, flying with its wings.[39]

The minor tension between Aten being the 'sole god' and the remark that 'like whom there is no other', can be read as an indication that the Aten-religion though monotheistic in outline did accept the existence of other deities. The area in which Aten is seen as incomparable, is his power to create heaven and earth.

In the Ugaritic texts, the theme of divine incomparability is absent.[40] The gods, however, are not seen as completely equal to each other. Of Baal it is said:

> Our king is Baal, the almighty
>> Our judge, nobody is above him![41]

The god Ilu is presented as follows:

> Your decree is wise, O Ilu,
> Your wisdom is eternal,
> A fortunate life is your decree
> ...
> You are great, Ilu,
> you are so wise,
> Your grey beard instructs you.[42]

This short and certainly not complete or entire survey makes clear that the theme of divine incomparability is not restricted to a monotheistic belief-system. The impression is given by the various texts that incomparability is a label given to one god in a pantheon with a tendency to monolatrism.[43] This is certainly true for the hymn in Micah 7: the existence of other gods is not denied, but they fall short to the virtues of YHWH.

---

39 Great Hymn of Aten: 78–82; see Sandman, *Texts*, 93–96; Lichtheim, *Literature II*, 92–96.
40 See Labuschagne, *Incomparability*, 62–63.
41 *KTU* 1.3 v: 32.
42 *KTU* 1.4 iv: 41–43; 1.4 v: 3–4; see Lewis, *Origin and Character of God*, 78–79.
43 Middlemas, *Divine image*, 93–04

6 Papyrus Amherst 63: Three Yahwistic Hymns

The Israelite section of papyrus Amherst 63 contains three hymns:[44]
- xii:11–19   probably a precursor of the Biblical Psalm 20;[45]
- xiii:1–10   a song celebrating the joy of the New Moon festival;[46]
- xiii:11–17   a hymn on Yahô as an incomparable divine and empathic warrior.[47]

According to Van der Toorn, these three hymns belong together. He reads them as parts of a New Year Festival. In his view, the elements of the 'new wine', the 'New Moon', and the enthronement in the heavenly council hint – in combination – to the celebration of an autumnal New Year.[48] His view is interesting, but based on an overinterpretation of the hymns. 'Wine' – y'yn', יין, is mentioned in the second song,[49] but is not presented as 'new wine' and a connection with the theme of harvest is absent. The song only states 'They have mixed the wine in our jars!' In line 7 b'ḥdyš'n', בחדישן, 'at our New Moon festival', is mentioned.[50] The New Moon was a monthly calendrical festival in Canaan and Ancient Israel.[51] Van der Toorn too quickly assumes a connection with the Ugaritic New Moon festival 'Beginning of the wine' in the twelfth month to argue that the song in papyrus Amherst 63 is connected with a New Year Festival.[52] Even if a connection to that festival could be made, it should be noted that the twelfth month is the last month of a year that should not be confused with the first month of the year. The hymn on Yahô as a divine warrior is praising God for his incomparability and will be discussed in the next section.

---

44 See Van der Toorn, *Papyrus Amherst 63*, 66–68 (text and translation), 165–75 (commentary).
45 See Vleeming, Wesselius, "Aramaic Hymn", 501–09; Zevit, "Common Origin"; Prinsloo, "Psalm 20"; Rösel, "Israels Psalmen in Ägypten", 86–90; Nims, Steiner, "Paganized Version"; Heckl, "Inside the Canon"; Van der Toorn, "Celebrating the New Year", 634–37.645–49 (with extensive literature); Van der Toorn, "Psalm 20", 244–61; Kister, "Psalm 20".
46 Kottsieper, "Anmerkungen"; Rösel, "Israels Psalmen in Ägypten", 93–96; Van der Toorn, "Celebrating the New Year", 637–43.
47 Kottsieper, "Anmerkungen"; Rösel, "Israels Psalmen in Ägypten", 96–97; Van der Toorn, "Celebrating the New Year", 643–45.
48 Van der Toorn, "Celebrating the New Year".
49 Pap Amherst 63 xiii:6.
50 See Van der Toorn, *Papyrus Amherst 63*, 171, who refers to a variety of other possible translations.
51 See e.g. Psalm 81.4; there exists much literature on this Canaanite/Israelite festival.
52 See Van der Toorn, *Papyrus Amherst 63*, 172; for the Ugaritic festival see Pardee, *Ritual and Cult*, 56–65.

7 A Hymn on the Incomparable God

The hymn can be translated as follows:
a. Who among the gods,
      among humankind, Yahô,
b. who among the gods,
      among king and non-king,
c. who is like you, Yahô,
      among the gods?
d. Out of protection, my Lord, take revenge
      Your worshippers, from the generations.
e. Take note of those who pursue us
      and restore and strengthen me.

f. Beneath you, Yahô
      beneath you, my Lord,
g. The host of heaven is as sand.
h. Yahô, the host of heaven
      proclaims to us your rule.
i. Take note of those who pursue us
      and restore and strengthen me.

j. Baal from Zaphon
      may bless Yahô.
k. Arise, Yahô, to our rescue.
l. Let his ears turn
      to the prayer, Lord.
m. arise Yahô!
n. Will you protect,
      as you have been protecting
        your people from days of old.[53]

Notes on the translation:
a. Van der Toorn reads m', מי a Hebraism for Aramaic מן, 'who'.[54] This Hebraism fits the Israelite section. Steiner, however, reads מן.[55]

---

53 pAmh 63 xiii:11–17.
54 Van der Toorn, *Papyrus Amherst 63*, 173.
55 Steiner and Nims, Aramaic Text in Demotic Script, 48.

The name of the God of Israel is written here – as elsewhere in pAmh – as HRᵍ.[56]

The word b'd'm, באדם, 'among humankind', is construed as the noun אדם in its collective meaning preceded by a preposition. This noun is not attested elsewhere in Aramaic and hence can be construed as a Hebrew loanword.

b. The words b'm'lk' | bl | m'lk', מלכא בל מלכא, is clearly an idiomatic expression for 'among king and commoner' and a merism for the whole of humankind.[57]

d. Both Steiner and Van der Toorn read mnnšrw 'dny but construe the words differently: as a topographical indication 'come from Shur',[58] or as an indication of time 'From the very beginning, Adonay'.[59] In my view, the noun שׁר should be taken in connection with the Aramaic noun שׁור, 'protective wall'.[60] It might be that in the present context, the aspect of protection has become important leading to a translation 'Out of protection, my Lord, take revenge', indicating that the 'worshippers' felt as in dire straits and was in need of divine protection.

The word n₂'q'm, נקם, should be construed as an imperative of the G-stem of the verb נקם.[61]

The noun d₅ry.C is a cognate of Hebrew דר, 'generation'.

e. The word by'n, בין, is an imperative m.s. of the verb בין, 'to understand', with the connotation of 'to have insight in; knowledge of'.[62]

The word "q'b'n, עקבן, is to be seen as a participle of the verb עקב, 'to pursue', with a suffix 1.c.p.[63]

The next line starts with another imperative: w't'b, ותב, 'do return', from the Aramaic verb תוב, a cognate of Hebrew שׁוב.

The second word in this line, w'n'ny, ואני, is construed by Steiner and van der Toorn as a noun with a suffix 'my strength; force'.[64] This is certainly

---

56 See on this Rösel, "Israels Psalmen in Ägypten", 90–91.

57 See also the Ugaritic Baal-epic *KTU* 1.4 vii:43–44; with Steiner, and Nims, Aramaic Text in Demotic Script, 49; Van der Toorn, *Papyrus Amherst 63*, 173. On merisms see Krašovec, *Merismus*.

58 Steiner and Nims, Aramaic Text in Demotic Script, 49.

59 Van der Toorn, *Papyrus Amherst 63*, 173; following Vleeming, Wesselius, *Studies in Papyrus Amherst 63*, 75.

60 See *TADAE* D5:6; *KAI* 202 A:10; pAmh xii:10; xx:9; xxii:1.6.7.15.

61 Steiner, and Nims, Aramaic Text in Demotic Script, 49; Van der Toorn, *Papyrus Amherst 63*, 173; on the semantic variety of this verb see Peels, *Vengeance*.

62 Cf. Van der Toorn, *Papyrus Amherst 63*, 174; against Steiner and Nims, Aramaic Text in Demotic Script, 49, who takes the word as a preposition and renders "a people dwelling among the crooked". The repetition of imperatives is an argument in favor of the view by Van der Toorn.

63 Van der Toorn, *Papyrus Amherst 63*, 174; the verb is also attested in Punic.

64 Steiner, and Nims, Aramaic Text in Demotic Script: 49; Van der Toorn, *Papyrus Amherst 63*, 174.

possible, but the connecting *wāw* does not suggest an object to the verb but another imperative.

g. In Phoenician, Punic, and Hebrew the noun d'r₂', דר, can have the meaning 'group of individual belonging together'.[65] In Ugaritic the expression *dr dt šmm*, 'the council of heaven', stands parallel to 'the assembly of the stars' and 'the sons of Ilu', all indicating a group of relatively minor deities.[66] Steiner construes a form of the Aramaic verb דאר, 'to dwell', and renders with 'resident of heaven'.[67] This proposal is less convincing.

The noun k'ḥ'w₂l', כחול, consist of a preposition and a noun. Steiner proposes to translate the noun חול with 'phoenix'.[68] This proposal is problematical for various reasons. (1) It would introduce the concept of revivication after death as known in Greek mythology into a much older text. (2) The translation of the Hebrew noun חול with 'phoenix' in Job 29:18 is far from certain.[69] A translation of חול with 'sand', is much more obvious.[70] The comparison of the 'host of heaven' with sand probably refers to the multitude of these deities.[71]

h. The word m'r₂'t'k', מרתך, 'your rule', is the object of the proclamation by the 'host of heaven'. The noun is connected to the Aramaic word מר, 'Lord', and indicates the sovereign rule of Lord Yahô.[72]

k. The word l'yl'n, לאילן, consists of a noun with a suffix 1.c.p. precede by a preposition. The noun איל – known from later Aramaic texts[73] – is not attested in Official Aramaic. Its Syriac, *'iyala*, and Hebrew, אֱיָל,[74] cognates – both meaning 'help' suggest a meaning 'help; rescue'.[75]

---

65 *DNWSI* 258–59.

66 *KTU* 1.10 i:3–5; see Kottsieper, "El – ferner oder naher Gott", 57; Van der Toorn, *Papyrus Amherst 63*, 174; 2019: 103.

67 Steiner and Nims, Aramaic Text in Demotic Script, 49.

68 Steiner and Nims, Aramaic Text in Demotic Script, 49.

69 See Van den Broek in *DDD*²: 655–57.

70 With Van der Toorn, *Papyrus Amherst 63*, 174.

71 With Van der Toorn, *Papyrus Amherst 63*, 174, who refers to the promise to Abraham in Gen. 22,17 "I will surely bless you and make your descendants as numerous as the stars in the sky and as the sand on the seashore."

72 Van der Toorn, *Papyrus Amherst 63*, 173; the rendition by Steiner, and Nims, Aramaic Text in Demotic Script: 50: 'your words', is probably prompted by the Biblical Psalm 19:1–5, where the heavens are seen as proclaiming the divine message; see Kottsieper, "El – ferner oder naher Gott", 57–60.

73 In Qumran and Rabbinic texts.

74 Psalm 88:5; 4Q216 2:9.

75 Steiner and Nims, Aramaic Text in Demotic Script, 50; Van der Toorn, *Papyrus Amherst 63*, 174.

l. The verb שׁוּב, 'return', is a Hebraism for Aramaic תוב.[76]
    The noun אדן is the Aramaic cognate of Hebrew אֹזֶן, 'ear'.
    The word t3'sl't', צלת, 'prayer', is clearly connected with the Hebrew and
    Aramaic verb צלה, 'to pray'.[77]

n. The verbform t'n'ṭ'r', תנטר,[78] is to be construed as a jussive 2.m.s. of the verb
    נטר, 'to protect'.[79]

8 With Whom and Why: Aspects of Divine Incomparability in the Extra Biblical Hymn

The hymn in Papyrus Amherst 63 stresses the character of the incomparability of
Yahô along two lines: with whom can this deity not be compared and what virtues
or acts make the deity so radically different? Both dimensions will be discussed.

8.1 With Whom?

The hymn opens with a twofold and repeated question. Two groups of individuals
are seen as incomparable with Yahô:
1. Divine beings and
2. Human beings.

The divine beings are not further specified by names or roles. The only gods that
are named in the hymn is the deity Baal and the collective of the 'host of heaven'.
The deity Baal is cast here in a supreme role who is invoked to bless Yahô.[80] This
means that Baal is in a position to empower Yahô and to improve the impending
acts of this deity. The 'host of heaven' are seen as a collective body of lower rank.
Their role is that of a messenger deity.[81] They only have to proclaim the rule of
Yahô.

As regards human beings, the hymn elaborates on the collective אדם with a
non-marked merism: 'king and commoner'. In my view, this implies that for the

---

76 Van der Toorn, *Papyrus Amherst 63*, 174.
77 See Van der Toorn, *Papyrus Amherst 63*, 174.
78 The /k/ at the end of the word is due to dittography with the first sign of the next line, see
Van der Toorn, *Papyrus Amherst 63*, 174.
79 Van der Toorn, *Papyrus Amherst 63*, 174; the verb is attested both in Aramaic and in Biblical
Hebrew: Song of Songs 1:8; Amos 1:11; Nahum 1:2.
80 On the semantic field of the verb ברך, see Leuenberger, *Segen*.
81 Handy, *Host of Heaven*, 149–68.

author of this hymn all of mankind – from the highest ruler to the most unimportant citizen – lack the power and the possibilities of Yahô.

8.2 Why?

The hymn makes a distinction between twee groups of divine acts:
1. Acts of protection since olden days
2. Impending acts of rescue and restoration.

The former protective acts of God are mentioned in element (n.). They are not enumerated or summarized. To the deity as well to the primary audience these acts must have been known. They function as an appeal to God: as you acted in the past, act in the near future.[82] What the supplicants hope for is that God will take revenge, protect and restore. Remarkably, these verbs have no objects. The first object, however, is immediately clear from the literary context. The supplicants pray to God that the deity would revenge them, protect them and restore them. The second object is less clear within the text. In the reality it must have been obvious which powers had brought the supplicants into despair and dire straits. The fact that they are not mentioned makes that the hymn can be appropriated in later comparable situations.

9 Do Not Put Your Trust in Princes, in Human Beings, Who Cannot Save (Psalm 146: 3)

The Aramaic hymn under discussion reflects a belief in Yahô comparable to the 'god-talk'in the closing hymn of the book of Micah. Both texts present the deity as incomparable to other deities and who is beyond and above all human powers. This image is the foundation of trust in times of trouble in the uncertainty before the reign of Josiah, in the diaspora in the oasis in the desert where the hymn was composed as well as in the Egyptian context in the fourth century when the hymn was written down in Demotic script.[83]

---

82 See Sanders, "Argumenta ad deum".
83 And I would add: עד היום הזה.

Two Additions to DDD

1 Introduction

When Karel van der Toorn, Pieter van der Horst, and myself were designing the *Dictionary of Deities and Demons in the Hebrew Bible*, we soon agreed on five categories of divine beings to be included:
1. Deities mentioned by name in the Bible (e.g. Baal; Zeus)
2. Gods occurring as theophoric element in personal or topographic names (for instance Bes)
3. Demythologized deities, i.e. Hebrew or Greek nouns that as such refer to a divine being in other cultures (Moon, Eros etc.)
4. Speculated deities, i.e. deities whose name is seen in Hebrew or Greek words (for instance Ra and Osiris)
5. Person who were deified in later traditions (Moses, Elijah, Maria and some others).

In view of the fourth category, we read through an abundance of secondary in the hope to scan all proposed deities and in the certainty that we would have missed a few. One divine being we missed was the one proposed by Saracino. In 1983 he had proposed to translated *nesîkê 'ādām* in Micah 5,4 not with the usual 'leaders of men' (NAS) but with biters (tormentors) of men' interpreting these biters as demonic powers and suggesting that *'ādām* would not refer to a person but to the 'earth' in the sense of the 'netherworld'.[1] As an extra argument, he remarks that 'The demon >biter< is recurrent in Akkadian magical literature'[2] and present a set of parallels from the Ugaritic literature.

His proposal has been adopted by Wagenaar who added three remarks.[3] First, he reinforces the view of Gordon that Mic. 5,4b-5 should be read as an incantation for the moment the Assyrian army would enter the territory of Judah. Second, he presents a Mesopotamian incantation in which a demon is said to have bitten a rival demon.[4] Third, he expands the proposal of Saracino by suggesting that *ro'îm* in the previous line should also be construed as referring to a crowd of demons and not to a groups of shepherds.

If ever a third edition of *DDD* would see the light of day, the following two entries need to be included.

---

1 Saracino, "State of Siege", esp. 266.
2 Saracino, "State of Siege", 266.
3 Wagenaar, *Judgement and Salvation*, 284–300.
4 LB 2001; see de Liagre Böhl, "Zwei altbabylonische Beschwörungstexte".

https://doi.org/10.1515/9783111208657-014

Biters נסיכים

I. The noun נסיכים in Micah 5:4b, should not – as usual – be rendered with 'leaders', but as a reference to a crowd of biting demons that keep the enemy at a distance.

II. The identity of these biters is unclear. They had demonic and apotropaic powers and were probably theriomorph. In Mesopotamian texts, the verb *našāku*, 'to bite', often has 'wild or rabid animals' as its subject (*CAD N/2*, 54). For instance in the incantation LB2001:3 'with his teeth he was grabbed and he grabbed him, where his rival had bitten (*iš-šu-ku*), he doubted his evil' (de Liagre Böhl 1954; Wagenaar 2001: 185). In the ritual text KAR 298 rev. 17 the names of two apotropaic dogs are mentioned: 'Do-Not-Deliberate-Open-Your-Mouth' and 'Do-Not-Deliberate-Bite (*ú-šuk*). These text reinforce the idea that 'biters' should be seen as angry animals with the power to keep the enemy at a distance.

In Ugaritic texts, the [n]tk, 'Biter', is attested in an anthology of incantations with a section in which the Sun-deity is summoned to collect various threatening entities among which: 'from the mouth of the [B]iter the destruction; from the mouth of the Devourer the destruction' (KTU 1.107:44–45; see de Moor 1981:113; Wagenaar 2001: 185–86; del Olmo Lete 2013). 'Biter' and 'Devourer' are to be read as names for demons.

III. Micah 5:4b-5 is to be seen as an incantation. The textual unit shows similarities with North-West Semitic incantations (Saracino 1983; Gordon 1991). This implies that the noun נסיכים in Micah 5:4b can preferably be seen as referring to a crowd of apotropaic theriomorph demons (Wagenaar 2001: 184–86). They are mentioned parallel to → 'breakers'.

IV. *Bibliography*

R. P. GORDON, "*K/ki/ky* in Incantional Incipits." *UF* 23 (1991), 161–63; F. M. Th. DE LIAGRE BÖHL, „Zwei altbabylonische Beschwörungstexte: LB 2001 und 1001 (Tafel II)", *BiOr* 11 (1954), 81–83; J. C. DE MOOR, "Demons in Canaan", *JEOL* 27 (1981), 106–19; G. DEL OLMO LETE, "KTU 1.107: A miscellany of incantations against snakebite", *UF* 44 (2013), 193–204; F. SARACINO, "A State of Siege: Mi 5 4–5 and an Ugaritic Prayer", *ZAW* 95 (1983), 263–69; J. A. WAGENAAR, *Judgment and Salvation: The Composition and Redaction of Micah 2–5* (VTSup 85), Leiden 2001.

Breakers רעים

I. The noun רעים in Micah 5:4b, should not – as usual – be rendered with 'shepherds', but as a reference to a bunch of demons that are breaking through the inimical lines.

II. The identity of these breakers is unclear. The Hebrew verb *rā'āh* V, 'to break' has no cognate in Akkadian or Ugaritic. A comparable word is also absent from the Westsemitic inscriptions.

III. Micah 5:4b-5 is to be seen as an incantation. The textual unit shows similarities with North-West Semitic incantations (Saracino 1983; Gordon 1991). Next to that, the word stands parallel to → 'breakers'. This implies that רעים should not be translated with the more neutral 'shepherds'. The suggestion to vocalise *rā'îm, 'evil spirits' (see Wagenaar 2001: 184), would fit within the interpretation that 5:4b-5 contains an incantation. The text would then refer to seven demons like the *sibitti* which are combatted in Akkadian incantations. The plural for *rā'āh*, 'evil one', however, would be *rā'ôt*. I therefore propose to render with a form of the verb *rā'āh* V, 'to break' (*DCH* VII: 521; the verb is probably also attested at Job 24:21; Gordis 1978: 270). In sum: these 'breakers' are demonic powers that could disrupt the advancing enemy.

IV. *Bibliography*

R. GORDIS, *The book of Job: Commentary, New Translation and Special Studies.* New York 1978; R. P. GORDON, *"K/ki/ky* in Incantional Incipits." *UF* 23 (1991), 161–63; F. SARACINO, "A State of Siege: Mi 5 4–5 and an Ugaritic Prayer", *ZAW* 95 (1983), 263–69; J. A. WAGENAAR, *Judgment and Salvation: The Composition and Redaction of Micah 2–5* (VTSup 85), Leiden 2001.

Bibliography

Ackerman, Suzan, "Why is Miriam also among the Prophets? (And is Zipporah among the Priests?)," *JBL* 121 (2002), 47–80.

Ackerman, Suzan, *Women and the Religion of Ancient Israel* (YABRL), New Haven and London 2022.

Albertz, Rainer, "Hintergrund und Bedeutung des Elterngebots im Dekalog", *ZAW* 90 (1978), 348–74.

Albertz, Rainer, "Konfliktschlichtung durch Machtverzicht – Jesaja 2,2–5 auf den Hintergrund der alttestamentlichen Kriegs- und Friedenstraditionen", in: R. Albertz (Her.), *Der Mensch als Hüter seiner Welt* (CTB 16), Stuttgart 1990, 114–31.

Albertz, Rainer, *Religionsgeschichte Israels in alttestamentlicher Zeit* (GAT, 8/1–2), Göttingen 1992.

Albertz, Rainer, "Deuteronomistic History and the Heritage of the Prophets", in: M. Nissinen (ed.), *Congress Volume Helsinki 2010* (VT Sup 148), Leiden 343–67.

Albertz, Rainer, James D. Nogalski and Jacob Wöhrle (eds), *Perspectives on the Formation of the Book of the Twelve: Methodological Foundations-Redactional Processes-Historical Insights* (BZAW 433), Berlin and New York, 2012.

Albertz, Rainer, and Rüdiger Schmitt, *Family and Household Religion in Ancient Israel and the Levant*, Winona Lake 2012.

Andersen, Francis I., and D. Noel Freedman, *Micah: A New Translation with Introduction and Commentary* (AB 24E), New York 2000.

Arneth, Martin, "Möge Šamaš dich in das Hirtenamt über die vier Weltgegenden einsetzen": der "Krönungshymnus Assurbanipals" (SAA III,11) und die Solarisierung des neuassyrischen Königtums", *ZAbR* 5 (1999), 28–53.

Asad, Talal, *Genealogies of Religion: Discipline and Reasons of Power in Christianity and Islam*, London: Johns Hopkins University Press, 1993.

Bail, Ulrike, *"Die verzogene Sehnsucht hinkt an ihren Ort": Literarische Überlebensstrategien nach der Zerstörung Jerusalems im Alten Testament*, Gütersloh 2004.

Banister, Jamie A., *The God of Thunder and War in Micah, Habakkuk, and Zechariah* (Gorgias Biblical Studies, 68), Piscataway 2018.

Barstad, Hans M., *The Religious Polemics of Amos: Studies in the Preaching of Am 2, 7B-8; 4, 1–13; 5, 1–27; 6, 4–7; 8, 14* (VT Sup, 34), Leiden 1984.

Barstad, Hans M., "No Prophets? Recent Developments in Biblical Prophetic Research and Ancient Near Eastern Prophecy", *JSOT* 18 (1993), 39–60.

Barstad, Hans M., "The Understanding of the Prophets in Deuteronomy", *SJOT* 8 (1994), 236–51.

Barstad, Hans M., "Text-internal and Text-external Chronology in Jeremiah 31:31–34", *SEÅ* 61 (1996), 33–51.

Bauman, Zygmunt, *Society Under Siege*, Cambridge 2002.

Bauman, Zygmunt, *Does Ethics Have a Chance in a World of Consumers?* Cambridge, MA 2008.

Becking, Bob, *De ondergang van Samaria: Historische, exegetische en theologische opmerkingen bij II Koningen 17* (PhD Utrecht University), Meppel 1985.

Becking, Bob, "Expectations about the End of Time in the Hebrew Bible: Do they exist?", in: C. Rowland, J. Barton (eds.), *Apocalypticism in History and Tradition* (JSP Sup 43), Sheffield 2002, 44–59.

Becking, Bob, *Between Fear and Freedom: Essays on the Interpretation of Jeremiah 30–31* (OTS 51), Leiden 2004.

Becking, Bob, "The Boundaries of Israelite Monotheism", in: A. M. Korte, M. de Haardt (eds.), *The Boundaries of Western Monotheism: Interdisciplinary Explorations into the Foundations of Western Monotheism* (SThAR 13), Leiden 2008, 9–27.

https://doi.org/10.1515/9783111208657-015

Becking, Bob, "Means of Revelation in the Book of Jeremiah", in: H. M. Barstad and R. G. Kratz, *Prophecy in the Book of Jeremiah* (BZAW 388), Berlin and New York 2009, 33–47.

Becking, Bob, "The Ambivalence of Adaptation and the Ongoing Strength of Religion", in B. Becking (ed.), *Orthodoxy, Liberalism, and Adaptation: Essays on Ways of Worldmaking in Times of Change from Biblical, Historical and Systematic Perspectives* (SthAR 15), Leiden 2011, 271–76.

Becking, Bob, "Micah in Neo-Assyrian Light", in: R. P. Gordon, H. M. Barstad (eds), *"Thus speaks Ishtar of Arbela": Prophecy in Israel, Assyria, and Egypt in the Neo-Assyrian Period*, Winona Lake 2013, 111–128.

Becking, Bob, *Een dwarse dromer: Meedenken met Micha* (Woord op Zondag 14,8), Gorinchem 2013.

Becking, Bob, "Religious Polemics in the Book of Micah", in: R. Thelle, T. Stordalen and M. E. J. Richardson (eds), *New Perspectives on Old Testament Prophecy and History, FS Hans M. Barstad* (VTSup 168), Leiden 2015, 74–89.

Becking, Bob, "Prophetic Elements in Papyrus Amherst 63", in: V. Bachmann, A. Schellenberg, F. Ueberschar (eds), *Menschsein in Weisheit und Freiheit: Festschrift für Thomas Krüger* (OBO 296), Leuven 2022, 365–78.

Becking, Bob, and Marjo C. A. Korpel, "To Create, to Separate or to Construct: An Alternative for a Recent Proposal as to the Interpretation of the Verb ברא in Genesis 1:1–2:4a", *JHS* 10 (2010), # 3.

Benjamin, Don C., "An Anthropology of Prophecy", *Biblical Theology Bulletin* 21 (1991), 135–44.

Ben Zvi, Ehud, "Wrongdoers, Wrongdoing and Righting Wrongs in Micah 2", *Biblical Interpretation* 7 (1999), 87–99.

Ben Zvi, Ehud, *Micah* (FOTL 21B), Grand Rapids Cambridge UK 2000.

Blenkinsopp, Joseph, *A history of prophecy in Israel* (Second revised and enlarged edition), Louisville 1996.

Blenkinsopp, Joseph, "Remembering Josiah", in: E. Ben Zvi and D. V. Edelman (eds), *Remembering Biblical Figures in the Late Persian and Early Hellenistic Periods: Social Memory and Imagination*, Oxford 2013, 236–56.

Block Daniel I., *The Gods of the Nations: Studies in Ancient Near Eastern Theology* (ETS), Grand Rapids 2000.

Boloje, Blessing O., "Trading Yahweh's Word for a Price: Ethical Implications of the Collusion of Prophets and Priests in Micah 3: 5–7, 11." *Old Testament Essays* 31 (2018), 630–50.

Bonhoeffer, Dietrich, *Ethik* (Herausg. von I. Tödt, H. E. Tödt, E. Feil und C. Green), Gütersloh 1949.

Boogaart, Thomas A., *Reflections on Restoration: A Study on Prophecies in Micah and Isaiah about the Restoration of Northern Israel* (Diss., Groningen, 1981).

Borger, Riekele, "Gott Marduk und Gott-König Šulgi als Propheten", *BiOr* 28 (1971), 3–24.

Bowen, Nancy R., "The Daughters of Your People: Female Prophets in Ezekiel 13:17–23", *JBL* 118 (1999), 417–33.

Bowie, Fiona, *The Anthropology of Religion*, Oxford 2000.

Brenner, Athalya, and Fokkelien van Dijk-Hemmes, *On Gendering Texts: Female and Male Voices in the Hebrew Bible* (BIS, 1), Leiden 1993.

Brettler, Marc Z, *The Metaphorical Mapping of God in the Hebrew Bible*, Duisburg 1997.

Brueggemann, Walter, *Theology of the Old Testament: Testimony, Dispute, Advocacy*, Minneapolis 1997.

Brueggemann, Walter, "Walk Humbly with your God: Micah 6:8", *Journal for Preachers* 33 (2010), 14–19.

Bruin, Wim M. de, "Reading the Book of Micah as Mediation Between Two Perspectives on the Enemy," in: J. van Ruyten, K. van Bekkum (eds), *Violence in the Hebrew Bible: Between Text and Reception* (OTS, 79), Leiden 315–37.

Buchanan, George W., "Eschatology and the 'End of Days'", *JNES* 20 (1961), 188–93.

Burkitt, Francis C., "Micah 6 and 7 a Northern Prophecy", *JBL* 45 (1926), 159–61.

Burnett, Joel S., ""Going Down" to Bethel: Elijah and Elisha in the Theological Geography of the Deuteronomistic History", *JBL* 129 (2010), 281–97.

Carroll, M. Daniel, ""He has told you what is good": Moral Formation in Micah", in: M. D. Carroll and J. E. Lapsley (eds), *Character ethics and the Old Testament: Moral Dimensions of Scripture* (Louisville, London: Westminster John Knox, 2007), 103–118.

Carroll, Robert P., "Night Without Vision: Micah and the Prophets", in: F. García Martínez, A. Hilhorst, C. J. Labuschagne (eds), *The Scriptures and the Scrolls* (FS A. S. van der Woude; VT Sup, 49), Leiden 1992, 74–84.

Cathcart, Kevin J., "Notes on Micah 5, 4–5", *Biblica* (1968), 511–14.

Chapman, Cynthia R., *The Gendered Language of Warfare in the Israelite-Assyrian Encounter* (HSM, 62), Winona Lake 2004.

Claassens, L. Juliana, and Irmtraut Fischer (eds), *Prophecy and Gender in the Hebrew Bible* (The Bible and Women: An Encyclopedia of Exegesis and Cultural History 1.2), Atlanta 2021.

Clifford, Hywell, "Deutero-Isaiah and Monotheism", in: J. Day (ed.) *Prophecy and Prophets in Ancient Israel: Proceedings of the Oxford Old Testament Seminar* (LHB/OTS 531), New York and London 2010, 267–289.

Clines, David J. A., "He-Prophets: Masculinity as a Problem for the Hebrew Prophets and Their Interpreters," in: D. J. A. Clines and Ph.R. Davies (eds.), *Sense and Sensitivity: Essays on Reading the Bible in Memory of Robert Carroll* (JSOTSup, 348), Sheffield 2002, 311–28.

Colonna, Marie-Laure, "Archétype/Image archétypique, la colère d'Ishtar", *Textes et contextes* 11 (2016), http://preo.u-bourgogne.fr/textesetcontextes/index.php?id=975 (consulted April 29, 2022).

Collins, Terence, *The Mantle of Elijah: The Redaction Criticism of the Prophetic Books* (Biblical Seminar 20), Sheffield 1993, 72–73.

Cooley, Jeffrey L., "The Story of Saul's Election (1 Samuel 9–10) in the Light of Mantic Practice in Ancient Iraq", *JBL* 130 (2011), 247–61.

Coppens, Joseph, *Les douze petits prophètes: bréviaire du prophétisme*, Louvain 1950.

Corzillius, Björn, *Michas Rätsel: Eine Untersuchung zur Kompositionsgeschichte des Michabuches* (BZAW 483), Berlin, New York 2016.

Cryer, Frederick C., *Divination in its Ancient Near Eastern Environment: A Socio–Historical Investigation* (JSOT Sup 142), Sheffield 1994.

Cruz, Juan, *"Who is like Yahweh?": a study of divine metaphors in the book of Micah* (FRLANT 263), Göttingen 2016.

Cuffey, Kenneth H., *The Literary Coherence of the Book of Micah: Remnant, Restoration, and Promise* (LHB/OTS 611), New York 2015.

Day, John, "Psalm 104 and Akhenaten's Hymn to the Sun", in: S. Gillingham (ed.), *Jewish and Christian Approaches to the Psalms: Conflict and Convergence*, Oxford 2013, 211–28.

Decorzant, Alain, *Vom Gericht zum Erbarmen: Text und Theologie von Micha 6–7*, Würzburg 2010.

Deden, Dirk, *De kleine profeten* (de Boeken van het Oude Testament), Roermond, Maaseik 1953.

Deller, Karl Heinz, "Die Briefe des Adad-šumu-Usur', in: M. Dietrich, W. Röllig (eds), *lišān mithurti* (FS W. von Soden; AOAT 1), Neukirchen-Vluyn 1969, 45–64.

Dempsey, Carol J., "Micah 2–3: Literary Artistry, Ethical Message, and Some Considerations About the Image of Yahweh and Micah", *JSOT* 85 (1999), 117–28.

Dempster, Stephen G., *Micah* (Two Horizons Old Testament Commentary), Grand Rapids 2017.

Deurloo, Karel A. en Machteld van Woerden, *Om het recht lief te hebben: verhalen over de boerenprofeet Micha*, Baarn 1983.

Dever, William G., *Did God Have a Wife? Archaeology and Folk Religion in Ancient Israel*, Grand Rapids and Cambridge, UK 2005.

Dietrich, Manfred, "Der Einbau einer Öffnung in den Palast Baals. Bemerkungen zu RS 94.2953 und KTU 1.4 VII 14–28", *UF* 39 (2007), 117–34.

Dietrich, Walter, *Prophetie und Geschichte: Eine redaktionsgeschichtliche Untersuchung zum deutero-nomistischen Geschichtswerk* (FRLANT, 108), Göttingen 1972.

Dietrich, Walter, "Einübung in den aufrechten Gang: Beispiele für Zivilcourage in den Samuelbüchern", in: M. C. A. Korpel, L. L. Grabbe (eds), *Openmidedness in the Bible and Beyond: A Volume of Studies in Honour of Bob Becking* (LHB/OTS 616), London, New York 2015, 57–67.

Di Fransisco, Lesley, ""He Will Cast their Sins into the Depths of the Sea..." Exodus Allusions and the Personification of Sin in Micah 7: 7–20", *VT* 67 (2017), 187–203.

Dreisbach, Daniel L., "Micah 6:8 in the Literature of the American Founding Era: A Note on Religion and Rhetoric", *Rhetoric an Public Affairs* 12 (2009), 91–105.

Ebeling, Erich, *Die akkadische Gebetsserie "Handerhebung"*, Berlin 1953.

Ebeling, Erich, "Ein Hymnus auf die Suprematie des Sonnengottes in Exemplaren aus Assur und Boghazköi", *Orientalia NS* 23 (1954), 209–16.

Edelkoort, Albertus H., *De Christusverwachting van het Oude Testament*, Wageningen 1941.

Edelkoort, Albertus H., *Micha de profeet vol recht en heldenmoed*, Baarn 1948.

Edelkoort, Albertus H., "Prophet and Prophets", *OT Studien* 5, Leiden 1948, 179–89.

Eissfeldt, Otto, „Ein Psalm aus Nord-Israel. Micha 7, 7–20", *ZDMG* 112 (1962), 259–68.

Enmarch, Roland, *The Dialogue of Ipuwer and the Lord of All* (Griffith Institute Publications), Oxford 2005.

Esztári, Réka, and Ádám Vér, "The Voices of Ištar," in: G. G. Xeravits (ed.), *Religion and Female Body in Ancient Judaism and Its Environments* (Deuterocanonical and Cognate Literature Studies, 28), Berlin and New York: De Gruyter, 2015, 3–40.

Falkenstein, Adam, *Sumerische Götterlieder* (Abhandlungen der Heidelberger Akademie der Wissenschaften, Phil.-hist. Kl., Jahrgang 1959, 1. Abh.), Heidelberg 1959.

Feil, Ernst, *Die Theologie Dietrich Bonhoeffers: Hermeneutik, Christologie, Weltverständnis* (6. Auflage), Münster 2005.

Ferry, Joëlle, *Illusions et salut dans la prédication prophétique de Jérémie* (BZAW 269), Berlin New York 1999.

Fohrer, Georg, „Micha 1", in: F. Maass (ed.), *Das Ferne und Nahe Wort: Festschrift Leonhard Rost*: (BZAW 105), Berlin, New York 1967, 65–80.

Foster, Benjamin R., *Before the Muses. An Anthology of Akkadian Literature*, Bethesda 2005.

Fritz, Volkmar, "Das Wort gegen Samaria Mi 1 2–7", *ZAW* 86 (1974), 316–31.

Frymer-Kensky, Tikva S., *In the Wake of the Goddesses: Women, Culture, and the Biblical Transformation of Pagan Myth*, New York 1992.

Fuchs, Esther, *Sexual Politics in the Biblical Narrative: Reading the Hebrew Bible as a Woman* (LHB/OTS, 310), Sheffield 2003.

Gafney, Wida C., *Daughters of Miriam: Women Prophets in Ancient Israel*, Minneapolis 2008.

Geertz, Clifford, "Religion as a Cultural System", in: M. Banton (ed.), *Anthropological Approaches to the Study of Religion* (ASA Monographs, 3), London 1966, 1–46.

Gesenius, Wilhelm, Ernst Kautzsch, Arthur E. Cowley, *Hebrew Grammar*, Oxford 1898.

Gilmour, Garth, "An Iron Age II Pictorial Inscription from Jerusalem Illustrating Yahweh and Asherah", *PEQ* 141 (2009), 87–103.

Goodman, Nelson, *Ways of Worldmaking*, Indianapolis 1978.

Grayson, A. Kirk, and Wilfred L. Lambert, "Akkadian Prophecies", *JCS* 18 (1964), 7–30.

Grey, Jacqueline, "Female Prophetic Traditions in the Old Testament: A Case Study of Isaiah's Woman (Isaiah 8.1–4)," *Journal of Pentecostal Theology* 30 (2021), 70–82.

Grollenberg, Lucas, „Micha 7: Eine Buss-Liturgie?", *Schrift* 17 (1971), 188–91.

Groot, Aart de, "Edelkoort, Albertus Hendrik", in: *Biografisch lexicon voor de geschiedenis van het Nederlands protestantisme* 4, Kampen 1998, 125–26.

Gruber, Mayer I, "Women's Voices in Micah", *Lectio Difficilior* 1 (2007), http://www.lectio.unibe.ch.

Gunkel, Herrmann, „Der Micha-Schluß. Zur Einführung in die literaturgeschichtliche Arbeit am AT", *ZS* 2 (1924), 145–78.

Hagedorn, Anselm C., *Die Anderen im Spiegel: Israels Auseinandersetzung mit den Völkern in den Büchern Nahum, Zefanja, Obadja und Joel* (BZAW 414), Berlin, New York 2012.

Hagstrom, David G., *The Coherence of the Book of Micah: A Literary Analysis* (SBLDS 89), Atlanta 1988.

Halton, Charles, "Allusions to the Stream of Tradition in Neo-Assyrian Oracles", *Ancient Near Eastern Studies* 46 (2009), 50–61.

Hamori, Esther J., *Women's Divination in Biblical Literature: Prophecy, Necromancy, and Other Arts of Knowledge* (YABRL), New Haven and London 2015.

Handy, Lowell K., *Among the Host of Heaven: The Syrian-Phoenician Pantheon as Bureaucracy*, Winona Lake 1994.

Hargrove, Barbara, *The Sociology of Religion: Classical and Contemporary Approaches*, Arlington Heights, IL 1979.

Harris, Rivkah, "Inanna-Ishtar as paradox and a coincidence of opposites." *History of Religions* 30 (1991), 261–78.

Harvey, Julien, *Le Plaidoyer prophétique contre Israel après la rupture de l'alliance*, Bruxelles 1967.

Heckl, Raik, "Inside the Canon and Out: The Relationship Between Psalm 20 and Papyrus Amherst 63", *Semitica* 56 (2014), 359–79.

Heiser, Michael, "Monotheism, Polytheism, Monolatry, or Henotheism? Toward an Assessment of Divine Plurality in the Hebrew Bible", *Bulletin for Biblical Research* 18 (2008), 1–20.

Helle, Sophus, ""Only in Dress?" Methodological Concerns Regarding Non-Binary Gender", in: S. Budin, M. Cifarelli, A. Garcia-Ventura, and A. Millet Albà (eds), *Gender and Methodology in the Ancient Near East: Approaches from Assyriology and beyond* (Barcino Monographica Orientalia, 10), Barcelona 2018, 41–53.

Hillers, Delbert R., *Treaty-Curses and the Old Testament Prophets* (BeO 16), Roma 1964.

Hillers, Delbert R., "*Hôy* and the *Hôy*-Oracles: A Neglected Syntactic Aspect," in: C. L. Meyers and M. P. O'Connor (eds), *The Word of the Lord Shall Go Forth*, Winona Lake 1983, 185–88.

Hillers, Delbert R., *Micah: A Commentary on the Book of the Prophet Micah* (Hermeneia), Philadelphia 1984.

Holm, Tawny L., *Aramaic Literary Texts* (SBL WAW), Atlanta 2023 [in press]

Holter, Knut, "Bildeforbudet i det gamle testament", *DIN-Tidsskrift for religion og kultur* 3–4 (2010), 28–44.

Hout, Cornelis F. M. van den, *Struikelblokken op de weg naar restauratie: Het boek Zacharia als dramatische tekst* (PhD Nijmegen), Maastricht 2009.

Hubbard, Robert L., "Micah, Moresheth, and Martin: Keep Up the Beat (Micah 6: 8)", *Covenant Quarterly* 65 (2007), 3–10.

Hume, David, "Commit It to the Flames", in: S. Baronett (ed), *Journey into Philosophy: An Introduction with Classic and Contemporary Readings*, New York 2016, 157–61.

Hutton, Jeremy M., "Local Manifestations of Yahweh and Worship in the Interstices: A Note on Kuntillet Ajrud", *Journal of Ancient Near Eastern Religions* 10 (2010), 177–210.

Hyatt, J. Philip, "On the Meaning and Origin of Micah 6:8", *Anglican Theological Review* 34 (1952), 232–39.

Hyman, Ronald T., "Questions and response in Michah 6:6–8", *JBQ* 33 (2005), 157–65.

Jacobs, Mignon R., *The Conceptual Coherence of the Book of Micah* (JSOT Sup 322; Sheffield: Sheffield Academic Press, 2001.
Jacobs, Mignon R., "Bridging the Times: Trends in Micah Studies since 1985", *Currents in Biblical Research* 4 (2006), 293–329.
Janzen, Waldemar, *Mourning Cry and Woe Oracle* (BZAW 125), Berlin und New York 1972.
Jeffers, Ann, *Magic and Divination in Ancient Palestine and Syria* (SHCANE 8), Leiden 1996.
Jensen, Joseph, *Ethical dimensions of the Prophets*, Collegeville 2006.
Jensen, Renée R., "Micah 4: 1–5", *Interpretation* 52 (1998), 417–20.
Jenson, Philip P., *Obadiah, Jonah, Micah: A Theological Commentary* (LHB/OTS, 496), New York, London 2008.
Jeppesen, Knud, "New Aspects of Micah Research", *JSOT* 8 (1978), 3–32.
Jeppesen, Knud, "How the Book of Micah lost its Integrity: Outline of the History of the Criticism of the book of Micah with Emphasis on the 19th century", *Studia Theologica* 33 (1979), 101–31.
Jeppesen, Knud, "Micah v 13 in the Light of a Recent Archaeological Discovery", *VT* 34 (1984), 462–66.
Jeremias, Jörg, *Theophanie: Die Geschichte einer alttestamentlichen Gattung* (WMANT 10), Neukirchen Vluyn 1965.
Jeremias, Jörg, „Die Deutung der Gerichtsworte Michas in der Exilszeit", *ZAW* 83 (1971), 330–54.
Jeremias, Jörg, „Tradition und Redaktion in Micha 3", in: A. Graupner e.a. (eds), *Verbindungslinien: Festschrift für Werner H. Schmidt zum 65. Geburtstag*, Neukirchen-Vluyn 2000, 137–51.
Jeremias, Jörg, *Die Propheten Joel, Obadja, Jona, Micha* (ATD, 24,3), Göttingen 2007.
Ji, Hyung-Won, "The rhetorical beauty and the socio-theological impact of Micah 6:6–8", in: Y.-M. Yi, Y. J. Yoo (eds), *Mapping and Engaging the Bible in Asian Cultures*, Seoul 2009, 195–211.
Jones, Barry A., *The Formation of the Book of the Twelve: A Study in Text and Canon* (SBL DS 149), Atlanta 1995.
Jong, Matthijs de, *Isaiah among the Ancient Near Eastern Prophets: A Comparative Study of the Earliest Stages of the Isaiah Tradition and the Neo-Assyrian Prophecies* (VT Sup 117), Leiden 2007.
Jong, Matthijs de, "'It Shall Be Night to You, without Vision': The Theme of Divine Disfavour in the Biblical Prophetic Books", in: B. Becking (ed.), *Reflections on the Silence of God: A Discussion with Marjo Korpel and Johannes de Moor* (OTS 62), Leiden 2013, 105–26.
Jong Ellis, Maria de, "Observations on Mesopotamian Oracles and Prophetic Texts: Literary and Historiographic Considerations", *JCS* 41 (1989), 140–57.
Joosten, Jan, "YHWH's Farewell to Northern Israel (Micah 6,1–8)", *ZAW* 125 (2013), 448–62.
Kämmerer, Thomas R., Kai A. Metzler, *Das babylonische Weltschöpfungsepos Enūma elîš* (AOAT 375), Münster 2012.
Kessler, Rainer, *Micha* (HThKAT), Freiburg 1999.
Kister, Menahem, "Psalm 20 and Papyrus Amherst 63: A Window to the Dynamic Nature of Poetic Texts", *VT* 70 (2019), 426–457.
Klein, Lilian R., *From Deborah to Esther: Sexual Politics in the Hebrew Bible*, Minneapolis 2003.
Knierim, Rolf, *The Task of Old Testament Theology: Substance, Method and Cases*, Grand Rapids, Cambridge 1995.
Konstantopoulos, Gina, "Women and the Interpretation of Dreams In Sumerian and Akkadian Literature," *JCS* 74 (2022), 89–108.
Korpel, Marjo C. A., and Johannes C. de Moor, *The Silent God*, Leiden, Boston 2011.
Kosmala, Hans, "At the End of the Days", *ASTI* 2 (1963), 27–37.
Kottsieper, Ingo, „Anmerkungen zu Pap. Amherst 63.I.12,11–19 – Eine Aramäische Version von Psalm 20", *ZAW* 100 (1988), 217–44.

Kottsieper, Ingo, "El – ferner oder naher Gott? Zur Bedeutung einer semitischen Gottheit in verschiedenen sozialen Kontexten im 1. Jtsd. v. Chr.", in: R. Albertz (ed.), *Religion und Gesellschaft* (AOAT 248), Münster: Ugarit-Verlag, 1997, 25–74.

Krašovec, Joze, *Der Merismus: im Biblisch-Hebraeischen und Nordwestsemitischen* (BeO, 130), Roma 1977.

Kratz, Reinhard G., "Theologisierung oder Säkularisierung? Der biblische Monotheismus im Spannungsfeld von Religion und Politik", in: O. Behrends (ed.), *Der biblische Gesetzesbegriff: Auf den Spuren einer Säkularisierung, 13. Symposion der Kommission "Die Funktion des Gesetzes in Geschichte und Gegenwart"* (AAWG.PH 278), Göttingen 2006, 43–67.

Kratz, Reinhard G. und Otto Merk, „Redaktionsgeschichte/Redaktionskritik I. Altes Testament II. Neues Testament", *TRE* 28 (1997), 367–378.378–384.

Kuhrt, Amelie, "The Cyrus Cylinder and Achaemenid Imperial Policy", *JSOT* 25 (1983), 83–97.

Labahn, Antje, *Wort Gottes und Schuld Israels* (BWANT 143), Stuttgart Berlin Köln 1999.

Labuschagne, Cas J., *The Incomparability of Yahweh in the Old Testament* (Pretoria Oriental Series 5), Leiden 1966.

Labuschagne, Cas J., "Opmerkelijke compositietechnieken in het Boek Micha", in: F. García Martínez, C. H. J. de Geus, A. F. J. Klijn (eds), *Profeten en profetische geschriften*, Kampen, Nijkerk 1985, 110–116.

Labuschagne, Cas J., *Numerical Secrets of the Bible: Rediscovering the Bible Codes*, North Richland Hills 2000.

Lang, Bernhard, *Der einzige Gott: Die Geburt des biblischen Monotheismus*, München 1981.

Lang, Bernhard, „Die Jahwe-allein-Bewegung: Neue Erwägungen über die Anfänge des biblischen Monotheismus", in: M. Oeming, K. Schmid (eds), *Der eine Gott und die Götter: Polytheismus und Monotheismus in antiken Israel* (ATANT 82), Zurich 2003, 97–110.

LeCureux, Jason T., *The Thematic Unity of the Book of the Twelve* (HBM 41), Sheffield 2012.

Leene, Henk, *De vroegere en de nieuwe dingen bij Deuterojesaja*, Amsterdam 1987.

Leene, Henk, "Jeremia 31,23–26 and the Redaction of the Book of Comfort", *ZAW* 104 (1992), 349–64.

Lemche, Nils Peter, "Did a Reform like Josiah's Happen?", in: P. R. Davies, D. V. Edelman (eds), *The Historian and the Bible Essays in Honour of Lester L. Grabbe* (LHB/OTS 530), New York and London 2010, 11–19.

Lescow, Thomas, „Redaktionsgeschichtliche Analyse von Micha 6–7", *ZAW* 84 (1972), 182–212.

Leuenberger, Martin, *Segen und Segenstheologien im alten Israel: Untersuchungen zu ihren religions- und theologiegeschichtlichen Konstellationen und Transformationen*, Zürich, 2008.

Levin, Christoph, *Die Verheißung des neuen Bundes in ihrem theologiegeschichtlichen Zusammenhang ausgelegt* (FRLANT 137), Göttingen 1985.

Levin, Christoph, „Das ‚Vierprophetenbuch'. Ein exegetischer Nachruf", *ZAW* 123 (2011), 221–35.

Lewis, Theodor J., *The Origin and Character of God: Ancient Israelite Religion through the Lens of Divinity*, Oxford 2020.

Liagre Böhl, Franz M. Th. de, „Zwei altbabylonische Beschwörungstexte: LB 2001 und 1001 (Tafel II)", *BiOr* 11 (1954), 81–83.

Lichtheim, Miriam, *Ancient Egyptian Literature, Volume II: The New Kingdom*, Berkeley 2006.

Longman, Tremper, *Fictional Akkadian Autobiography: A Generic and Comparative Study*, Winona Lake 1991.

Lundbom, Jack R., *Jeremiah 21–36: A New Translation with Introduction, Notes, and Commentary* (AB 21B), New York 2004.

Lyotard, Jean-François, *La condition postmoderne: rapport sur le savoir*, Paris 1979.

Maier, Christl M., "Feminist Interpretation of the Prophets," in: C. J. Sharp (ed), *The Oxford Handbook of the Prophets*, Oxford 2016, 467–74.

Marxsen, Willy, *Der Evangelist Markus. Studien zur Redaktionsgeschichte des Evangeliums* (FRLANT 67), Göttingen 1956.

Mastnjak, Nathan, *Deuteronomy and the Emergence of Textual Authority in Jeremiah* (FAT 2.87), Tübingen 2016.

Maul, Stefan M., *Die Wahrsagekunst im Alten Orient. Zeichen des Himmels und der Erde*, München 2013.

May, Nathaly N., "Women in Cult in First Millennium BCE Mesopotamia." In: K. De Graef, A. Garcia-Ventura, A. Goddeeris and B. Alpert Nakhai (eds), *The Mummy Under the Bed. Essays on Gender and Methodology in the Ancient Near East* (wEdge 1), Münster 2022, 125–56.

Mays, James L., *Micah* (OTL), London 1976.

McKane, William, *The Book of Micah: Introduction and Commentary* (ICC), Edinburgh 1998.

Mendez, Hugo E., *Condemnations of Necromancy in the Hebrew Bible: An Investigation of Rationale* (Diss. University of Georgia, 2009).

Mettinger, Tryggve N. D., *No Graven Image? Israelite Aniconism in its Ancient Near Eastern Context* (ConB OT, 42), Stockholm 1995.

Meyers, Carol L., Toni Craven and Ross S. Kraemer, *Women in Scripture: A Dictionary of Named and Unnamed Women in the Hebrew Bible, the Apocryphal/Deuterocanonical Books, and the New Testament*. Boston 2000.

Meyer, Esias E., "The particle כִּי, a mere conjunction or something more?", *JNSL* 27 (2001), 39–62.

Middlemas, Jill M., *The divine image: Prophetic aniconic rhetoric and its contribution to the aniconism debate* (FAT 74), Tübingen 2015.

Miller, Patrick D., *The Ten Commandments* (Interpretation), Louisville 2009.

Monroe, Lauren A. S., *Josiah's Reform and the Dynamics of Defilement: Israelite Rites of Violence and the Making of a Biblical Text*, Oxford 2011.

Moor, Johannes C. de, "Handschriften van de Hebreeuwse Bijbel", in: *Eeuwfeest-almanak van het Corpus Studiosorum in Academia Campensis "Fides Quaerit Intellectum"* 66, Kampen 1963, 143–58.

Moor, Johannes C. de, "Unit Division in the Peshitta of Micah", *JAB* 1 (1999), 225–247.

Moor, Johannes C. de, "Micah 7: 1–13: The Lament of a Disillusioned Prophet", in: M. Korpel, J. Oesch (eds), *Delimitation Criticism: A New Tool in Biblical Scholarship* (Pericope 1), Assen 2000, 149–96.

Moor, Johannes C. de, "The Structure of Micah 2: 1–13: The Contribution of the Ancient Witnesses", in: M. Korpel, J. Oesch (eds), *Studies in Scriptural Unit Division* (Pericope 3), Assen 2002, 90–120.

Moor, Johannes C. de, "The Structure of Micah 6 in the Light of Ancient Delimitations", in: M. Korpel, J. Oesch (eds), *Layout Markers in Biblical Manuscripts and Ugaritic Tablets* (Pericope 5), Assen 2005, 78–113.

Moor, Johannes C. de, *Micah*, HCOT, Leuven 2020.

Moor, Johannes C. de, and Marjo C. A. Korpel, *The Structure of Classical Hebrew Poetry: Isaiah 40–55* (OTS 41), Leiden 1998.

Mostovicz, E. Isaac, Nada K. Kakabadse, "He has told you, O man, what is good!," *Journal of Management Development* 31 (2012), 948–61.

Mowinckel, Sigmund, *Zur Komposition des Buches Jeremia*, Kristiana 1914.

Na'aman, Nadav, "The "Discovered Book" and the Legitimation of Josiah's Reform", *JBL* 130 (2011), 47–62.

Nasuti, Harry P., "The Once and Future Lament: Micah 2.1–5 and the Prophetic Persona", in: J. Kaltner, L. Stulman (eds), *Inspired Speech: Prophecy in the Ancient Near East Essays in Honor of Herbert B. Huffmon* (LHB/OTS, 378), London, New York: Continuum, 2004, 144–160.

Nelson, Richard D., *The Historical Books* (IBT), Nashville 1998.

Neujahr, Matthew, "Royal Ideology and Utopian Futures in the Akkadian ex eventu Prophecies", in E. ben Zvi (ed.), *Utopia and Dystopia in Prophetic Literature* (Publications of the Finnish Exegetical Society 92), Helsinki, Göttingen 2006, 41–54.

Newberry, Percy E., Walter E. Crum, *The Amherst Papyri, Being an Account of the Egyptian Papyri in the Collection of the Right Hon. Lord Amherst of Hackney, FSA, at Didlington Hall, Norfolk*, London 1899.

Newman, Louis E., "Balancing Justice and Mercy", *Journal of Religious Ethics* 41 (2013), 435–456.

Nicholson, Ernest W., "Deuteronomy 18.9–22, the Prophets and Scripture", in: J. Day (ed.) *Prophecy and Prophets in Ancient Israel: Proceedings of the Oxford Old Testament Seminar* (LHB/OTS 531), New York and London 2010, 151–71.

Nielsen, Kirsten, *YAHWEH as Prosecutor and Judge: An Investigation of the Prophetic Lawsuit (Rib-Pattern)* (JSOT Sup 9), Sheffield 1978.

Nims, Charles F., Richard C. Steiner, "A Paganized Version of Psalm 20:2–6 from the Aramaic Text in Demotic Script", *JAOS* 103 (1983), 261–74.

Nissinen, Martti, *References to Prophecy in Neo-Assyrian Sources* (SAAS, 7), Helsinki 1998.

Nissinen, Martti, "The Socio-Religious Role of the Neo-Assyrian Prophets." in: M. Nissinen (ed), *Prophecy in its Ancient Near Eastern Context: Mesopotamian, Biblical and Arabian Perspectives*, Atlanta 2000, 89–114.

Nissinen, Martti, *Prophets and Prophecy in the Ancient Near East*, with contributions by C. L. Seow and R. K. Ritner (SBLWAW, 12), Atlanta GA 2003.

Nissinen, Martti, "What is Prophecy? An Ancient Near Eastern Perspective", in: J. Kaltner and L. Stulman (eds), *Inspired Speech: Prophecy in the Ancient Near East Essays in Honor of Herbert B. Huffmon* (JSOT Sup 378), London and New York 2004, 17–37.

Nissinen, Martti, *Ancient Prophecy: Near Eastern, Biblical, and Greek Perspectives*, Oxford 2017.

Nissinen, Martti, "The Agency of Female Prophets in the Bible: Independent or Instrumental? Prophetic or Political?", in: K. Droß-Krüpe and S. Fink (eds), *Powerful Women in the Ancient World: Perception and (Self)Presentation, Proceedings of the 8th Melammu Workshop Kassel, 30 January – 1 February 2019* (Melammu Workshops and Monographs, 4), Münster 2021, 161–84.

Nissinen, Martti, and Marie-Claire Perroudon, "Bāia." in: J. D. Baker (ed), *The Prosopography of the Neo-Assyrian Empire* Vol. 2,I, Helsinki 2000, 253.

Nissinen, Martti, Choon-Leong Seow, Robert K. Ritner and H. Craig Melchert, *Prophets and Prophecy in the Ancient Near East* (Second Edition. SBLWAW, 41), Atlanta: Society of Biblical Literature, 2019.

Noegel, Scott B., *Nocturnal Ciphers: The Allusive Language of Dreams in the Ancient Near East* (AOS, 89), Winona Lake 2007.

Nogalski, Jame L., *Literary Precursors to the Book of the Twelve* (BZAW 217), Berlin, New York 1993.

Nogalski, Jame L., *Redactional Processes in the Book of the Twelve* (BZAW 218), Berlin, New York 1993.

Nogalski, Jame L., "Micah 7:8–20: Re-evaluating the Identity of the Enemy," in: R. Heskett, B. Irwin (eds.), *The Bible as a Human Witness to Divine Revelation: Hearing the Word of God Through Historically Dissimilar Traditions* (LHB/OTS, 469), London and New York 2007, 125–42.

O'Brien, Julia M., *Micah* (Wisdom Commentary, 37), Collegeville 2016.

Oesch, J., *Petucha und Setuma: Untersuchungen zu einer überlieferten Gliederung im hebräischen Text des Alten Testaments* (OBO 27), Göttingen, Freiburg 1979.

Olson, Dennis T., "God for Us, God against Us: Singing the Pentateuch's Songs of Praise in Exodus 15 and Deuteronomy 32", *Theology Today* 70 (2013), 54–61.

Olyan, Saul M., *Biblical Mourning: Ritual and Social Dimensions*, Oxford 2004.

Olyan, Saul M., "Unnoticed Resonances of Tomb Opening and Transportation of the Remains of the Dead in Ezekiel 37: 12–14", *JBL* 128 (2009), 491–502.

Olyan, Saul M., "Is Isaiah 40–55 Really Monotheistic?", *Journal of Ancient Near Eastern Religions* 12 (2012), 190–201.

Otto, Eckart, *Theologische Ethik des Alten Testaments* (ThW 3.2), Stuttgart 1994.

Paas, Stefan, "Bookends Themes? Maleachi, Hosea en het 'Boek van de Twaalf'", *NTT* 58 (2004), 1–17.

Pardee, Dennis, "The Many Faces of the Goddess: The Iconography of the Syro-Palestinian Goddesses Anat, Astarte, Qedeshet, and Asherah, c. 1500–1000 BCE", in: I. Cornelius, H. Niehr (eds), *Götter und Kulte in Ugarit: Kultur und Religion einer nordsyrischen Königsstadt in der Spätbronzezeit* (OBO 204), Fribourg und Göttingen 2009, 120–29.

Pardee, Dennis, *Ritual and Cult at Ugarit* (SBL WAW 10), Atlanta 2002.

Pardes, Ilana, *Countertraditions in the Bible: A Feminist Approach*, Cambridge 1992.

Park, Sung J., "The Cultic Identity of Asherah in Deuteronomistic Ideology of Israel", *ZAW* 123 (2011), 553–64.

Parpola, Simo, "The Forlorn Scholar", in: F. Rochberg-Halton (ed.), *Language, Literature, and History: Philological and Historical Studies Presented to Erica Reiner* (AOS 67), New Haven 1987, 257–78.

Parpola, Simo, *Assyrian Prophecies* (SAA, 9). Helsinki 1998.

Peacock, Kevin C., "Who is a God like you? Theological themes in Micah", *Southwestern Journal of Theology* 46 (2003), 27–47.

Peels, Eric H. G. L., *The Vengeance of God: The Meaning of the Root NQM and the Function of the NQM-texts in the Context of Divine Revelation in the Old Testament* (OTS, 31), Leiden 1994.

Penchansky, David, *Twilight of the Gods: Polytheism in the Hebrew Bible*, Louisville 2005.

Petersen, David L., *The prophetic literature: An introduction*, Louisville 2002.

Pfälzner, Peter, "The World of the Living and the World of the Dead", *German Research* 26 (2004), 16–20.

Philip, Lotte B., *The Ghent altarpiece and the art of Jan van Eyck*, Princeton 1971.

Pongratz-Leisten, Beate, *Herrschaftswissen in Mesopotamien: Formen der Kommunikation zwischen Gott und König im 2. und 1. Jahrtausend v. Chr.* (SAAS 10), Helsinki 1999.

Prinsloo, Gert T. M., "Psalm 20 and its Aramaic parallel: A Reappraisal", *JfS* 9 (1997), 48–86.

Pryke, Louise M., *Ishtar* (Gods and heroes of the Ancient World), Abingdon and New York 2017.

Redditt, Paul L., and Aaron Schart (eds), *Thematic Threads in the Book of the Twelve* (BZAW 325), Berlin and New York 2003.

Reiner, Erica, "Fortune-telling in Mesopotamia", *JNES* 19 (1960), 23–35.

Richelle, Matthieu, „Un triptyque au coeur du livre de Michée (Mi 4–5)", *VT* 62 (2012), 232–47.

Ridderbos, Jan, *De kleine profeten II: Obadja tot Zefanja* (Korte Verklaring), Kampen 1949.

Römer, Thomas C., *The So-called Deuteronomistic History: A Sociological, Historical and Literary Introduction*, London, New York 2005.

Rösel, Martin, "Israels Psalmen in Ägypten? Papyrus Amherst 63 und die Psalmen xx und lxxv", *VT* 50 (2000), 81–99.

Rogan, Johny, *The Byrds: Timeless Flight Revisited: the Sequel*, Leamington Spa, 1998.

Roth, M., *Israel und die Völker im Zwölfprophetenbuch: Eine Untersuchung zu den Büchern Joel, Jona, Micha und Nahum* (FRLANT 210), Göttingen 2005.

Rudman, Dominic, "Zechariah 8:20–22 & Isaiah 2:2–4//Micah 4:2–3: A Study in Intertextuality", *BN* 107/108 (2001), 50–54.

Runions, Erin, *Changing Subjects: Gender, Nation and Future in Micah* (Playing the Texts 7), Sheffield 2001.

Sanders, Paul, "Argumenta ad deum in the Plague Prayers of Mursili II and in the Book of Psalms", in: B. Becking, E. Peels (eds), *Psalms and Prayers* (OTS, 55), Leiden 2007, 181–217.

Sandman, Maj, *Texts from the Time of Akhenaten* (Bibliotheca Aegyptiaca 8), Bruxelles 1938.

Saracino, Francesco, "A State of Siege: Mi 5 4–5 and an Ugaritic Prayer", *ZAW* 95 (1983), 263–69.

Savran, George W., "Theophany as Type Scene", *Prooftexts* 23 (2003), 119–49.

Scaiola, Donatella, "The Twelve, one or many Books? A Theological Proposal." in: E. di Pede, D. Scaiola (eds), *The Book of the Twelve – One Book or Many?* (FAT 2, 91), Tübingen 2016, 180–93.

Schart, Aaron, *Die Entstehung des Zwölfprophetenbuchs: Neubearbeitungen von Amos im Rahmen schriftenübergreifender Redaktionsprozesse* (BZAW 260, Berlin, New York 1998.

Schmid, Konrad, *Buchgestalten des Jeremiabuches: Untersuchungen zur Redaktions- und Kompositionsgeschichte von Jer 30–33 im Kontext des Buches* (WMANT 72), Neukirchen-Vluyn 1996.

Schmidt, Brian B., *Israel's Beneficent Dead: Ancestor Cult and and Necromancy in Ancient Israelite Religion and Tradition*, Winona Lake 1994.

Schmidt, Ludwig, "Die alttestamentliche Bileamüberlieferung", *BiZs NF* 23 (1979), 234–61.

Schoors, Antoon, "The Particle כִּי", in: A. S. van der Woude (ed.), *Remembering all the way: A collection of Old Testament studies published on the occasion of the fortieth anniversary of the Oudtestamentisch Werkgezelschap in Nederland* (OTS 21), Leiden 1981, 240–76.

Schütte, Wolfgang, *Israels Exil in Juda: Untersuchungen zur Entstehung der Schriftprophetie* (OBO 279), Fribourg and Göttingen 2016.

Schultz, Richard L., *The Search for Quotation: Verbal Parallels in the Prophets* (JSOT Sup 180), Sheffield 1999.

Schuman, Niek A., *Micha* (Verklaring van een bijbelgedeelte), Kampen 1989.

Scriba, Albrecht, *Die Geschichte des Motivkomplexes Theophanie* (FRLANT 167), Göttingen 1995.

Sedlmeier, Franz, "Die Universalisierung der Heilshoffnung nach Micha 4,1–5", *Trierer Theologisches Zeitschrift* 107 (1998), 62–81.

Selms, Adrianus van, *Genesis deel I* (de Prediking van het Oude Testament), Nijkerk 1967.

Sjöberg, Åke W., "i n – n i n š à – g u r₄ – r a. A Hymn to the Goddess Inanna by the e n-priestess Enheduanna", *ZA* 65 (1975), 161–253.

Smith, Jonathan Z., *Imagining Religion: From Babylon to Jonestown*, Chicago 1982.

Smith, Morton, "The Common Theology of the Ancient Near East", *JBL* 71 (1952), 135–47.

Smith, Marc S., "The Blessing God and Goddess: A Longitudinal View from Ugarit to Yahweh and... his asherah at Kuntillet 'Ajrud", in: G. Eidevall and B. Scheuer (eds), *Enigmas and Images: Studies in Honor of Tryggve N. D. Mettinger* (ConB OT, 58), Winona Lake 2011, 206–19.

Smith, Ralph L., *Micah-Malachi* (WBC 32), Waco 1984.

Smith-Christopher, Daniel L., "Are the Refashioned Weapons in Micah 4:1–4 a Sign of Peace or Conquest? Shifting the Contextual Borders of a 'Utopian' Prophetic Motif", in E. ben Zvi (ed.), *Utopia and Dystopia in Prophetic Literature* (Publications of the Finnish Exegetical Society 92), Helsinki, Göttingen 2006, 186–209.

Sommer, Benjamin, *A Prophet Reads Scripture: Allusion in Isaiah 40–66*, Stanford 1998.

Spek, Robartus J. van der, "Cyrus the Great, Exiles and Foreign Gods: A Comparison of Assyrian and Persian Policies on Subject Nations", in: W. Henkelman, C. Jones, M. Kozuh and Chr. Woods (eds.), *Extraction and Control: Studies in Honor of Matthew W. Stolper* (Oriental Institute Publications), Chicago 2014, 233–64.

Stansell, Gary, *Micah and Isaiah: A Form and Tradition Historical Comparison* (SBL DS 85), Atlanta 1988.

Stavrakopoulou, Fransesca, *Land of Our Fathers: The Roles of Ancestor Veneration in Biblical Land Claims* (LHB/OTS 473), New York and London 2010.

Stavrakopoulou, Fransesca, *God: An Anatomy*, New York 2022.

Steiner, Richard C., Charles F. Nims, "You Can't Offer Your Sacrifice and Eat It Too: A Polemical Poem from the Aramaic Text in Demotic Script", *JNES* 43 (1984), 89–114.

Steiner, Richard C., Charles F. Nims, "Ashurbanipal and Shamash-shum-ukin: *A Tale of Two Brothers* from the Aramaic Text in Demotic Script", *RB* 92 (1985), 60–81.

Steiner, Richard C., Charles F. Nims, The Aramaic Text in Demotic Script: Text, Translation, and Notes, https://www.academia.edu/31662776/The_Aramaic_Text_in_Demotic_Script_Text_Translation_and_Notes [2017].

Steinert, Ulrike, "Ecstatic Experience and Possession Disorders in Ancient Mesopotamia.", in: D. L. Stein, S. K. Costello and K. Polinger Foster (eds.) *The Routledge Companion to Ecstatic Experience in the Ancient World*, Abingdon and New York 2021, 369–96.

Steymans, Hans U., *Deuteronomium 28 und die adê zur Thronfolgeregelung Asarhaddons: Segen und Fluch im Alten Orient und in Israel* (OBO 145), Freiburg, Göttingen, 1995.

Stökl, Jonathan, *Prophecy in the Ancient Near East: A Philological and Sociological Comparsion* (CHANE 56), Leiden 2012.

Stökl, Jonathan, "Gender "Ambiguity" in Ancient Near Eastern Prophecy? A Reassessment of the Data behind a Popular Theory," in: J. Stökl and C L. Carvalho (eds), *Prophets Male and Female: Gender and Prophecy in the Hebrew Bible, the Eastern Mediterranean and the Ancient Near East* (AIIL, 15), Atlanta 2013, 59–80.

Streck, Maximiliab, *Assurbanipal und die letzten assyrischen Könige bis zum Untergange Niniveh's,* (VAB VII), Leipzig 1916.

Strydom, Johannes G., *Micah, Anti-Micah and Deutero-Micah: A critical discussion with A S van der Woude* (Diss., Pretoria, 1988)."

Strydom, Johannes G., 'Micah of Samaria: Amos' and Hoshea's forgotten Partner', *OTE* 6 (1993), 19–32.

Sweeney, Marvin A., *The Twelve Prophets* (Berith Olam), Collegeville 2000.

Sweeney, Marvin A., "Micah's Debate with Isaiah", *JSOT* 93 (2001), 111–24.

Talon, Philip, *Enūma Eliš: The Standard Babylonian Creation Myth* (SAACT, 4), Helsinki 2005.

Talstra, Eep, *Solomon's Prayer: Synchrony and Diachrony in the Composition of I Kings 8, 14–61,* Kampen 1993.

Tietz, Christiane, *Dietrich Bonhoeffer: Theologe im Widerstand* (Becks Wissen, 2775), München 2013.

Toorn, Karel van der, "In the Lion's Den: The Babylonian Background of a Biblical Motif", *CBQ* 60 (1998), 626–40.

Toorn, Karel van der, *Scribal Culture and the Making of the Hebrew Bible*, Cambridge MA and London 2007.

Toorn, Karel van der, "Turning Tradition into Eternal Truth: The Invention of Revelation", *Studia Theologica Nordic Journal of Theology* 67 (2013), 3–27.

Toorn, Karel van der, "Celebrating the New Year with the Israelites: Three Extrabiblical Psalms from Papyrus Amherst 63", *JBL* 136 (2017), 633–49.

Toorn, Karel van der, "Psalm 20 and Amherst Papyrus 63, XII, 11–19: A Case Study of a Text in Transit", in: F. E. Greenspahn, G. A. Rendsburg (eds), *Le-maʿan Ziony: Essays in Honor of Ziony Zevit*, Eugene 2017, 244–61.

Toorn, Karel van der, *Papyrus Amherst 63* (AOAT 448), Münster 2018.

Torrance, Thomas F., "The Prophet Micah and his Famous Saying", *Evangelical Quarterly* 24 (1952), 206–14.

Tsukimoto, Akio, *Untersuchungen zur Totenpflege (kispum) im alten Mesopotamien* (AOAT 216), Kevelaer und Neukirchen-Vluyn 1985.

Utzschneider, Helmut, *Michas Reise in die Zeit: Studien zum Drama als Genre der prophetischen Literatur des Alten Testaments* (SBS 180), Stuttgart 1999.

Valdez, Stephen, "Folk Rock", in: L. Henderson, L. Stacey (eds), *Encyclopedia of Music in the 20th Century*, London 2014, 223.

Vleeming, Sven P., Jan-Wim Wesselius, "An Aramaic Hymn from the Fourth Century B.C.", *BiOr* 39 (1982), 501–09.

Vos, Dirk de, *De Vlaamse Primitieven; de meesterwerken*, Amsterdam 2002.

Vries, Simon J. de, *Bible and Theology in the Netherlands* (second edition), New York, Bern, Frankfurt/M., Paris 1989.

Vriezen, Theodoor C., *Oud-Israëlitische geschriften*, Den Haag 1948.

Vriezen, Theodoor C., *De literatuur van Oud-Israël*, Den Haag ²1961.

Vriezen, Theodoor C. en Adam S. van der Woude, *De literatuur van Oud-Israël*, Wassenaar ⁴1973; Katwijk ⁶1980.

Vriezen, Theodoor C. en Adam S. van der Woude, *Oudisraelitische en vroegjoodse literatuur*, Kampen ¹⁰2001.

Vriezen, Theodoor C. en Adam S. van der Woude, *Ancient Israelite and Early Jewish Literature*, Leiden 2005.

Wagenaar, Jan A., *Oordeel en heil: Een onderzoek naar samenhang tussen de heils- en onheilsprofetieën in Micha 2–5* (PhD Utrecht), 1995.

Wagenaar, Jan A., *Judgment and Salvation: The Composition and Redaction of Micah 2–5* (VTSup 85), Leiden 2001.

Wagner, Volker, *Profanität und Sakralisierung im Alten Testament* (BZAW 351), Berlin und New York 2005.

Wal, Adrie J. O. van der, *Micah: A Classified Bibliography*, Amsterdam 1990.

Walsh, Lynda, *Scientists as Prophets: A Rhetorical Genealogy* Oxford 2013.

Waltke, Bruce K., *A Commentary on Micah*, Grand Rapids, Cambridge 2007.

Waltke, Bruce K., Michael P. O'Connor, *An Introduction to Biblical Hebrew Syntax*, Winona Lake 1990.

Weber, Max, *Politik als Beruf* (Elfte Auflage), Berlin 2010.

Weippert, Manfred, "'König, fürchte dich nicht!' Assyrische Prophetie im 7. Jahrhundert v. Chr.", *Orientalia Nova Series* 71 (2002), 1–54.

Wellhausen, Julius, *Die kleine Propheten übersetzt und erklärt*, Berlin ⁴1963.

Wells, Bruce, "The Cultic Versus the Forensic: Judahite and Mesopotamian Judicial Procedures in the First Millennium B.C.E.", *JAOS* 128 (2008), 205–32.

Werner, Wolfgang, „Micha 6, 8: eine alttestamentliche Kurzformel des Glaubens? Zum theologischen Verständnis von Mi 6, 8", *BiZs NF* 32 (1988), 232–48.

Wessels, Wilhelm, "YHWH, the God of new Beginnings: Micah's testimony", *HTS Teologiese Studies / Theological Studies* 69 (2013), 1–8.

Westenholz, Joan G., "Inanna and Ishtar in the Babylonian World," in: G. Lecik (ed.), *The Babylonian World*, Abingdon 2007, 344–59.

Westermann, Claus, *Grundformen prophetischer Rede* (BEvTh 31), München 1964.

Williamson, Hugh G. M., *A Critical and Exegetical Commentary on Isaiah 1–5* (ICC), London 2014.

Willi-Plein, Ina, *Vorformen der Schriftexegese innerhalb des Alten Testaments: Untersuchungen zum literarischen Werden der auf Amos, Hosea und Micha zurückgehenden Bücher im hebräischen Zwölfprophetenbuch.* (BZAW 123), Berlin, New York 1971.

Willis, John T., "The Authenticity and Meaning of Micah 5 9–14", *ZAW* 81 (1969), 353–68.

Willis, John T., "A Reapplied Prophetic Hope Oracle", in: P. A. H. de Boer (ed.), *Studies on Prophecy* (VT Sup 26), Leiden 1974, 64–76.

Willis, John T., "The Expression *be'acharith hayyamin* in the Old Testament", *Restoration Quarterly* 22 (1979), 54–71.

Wilson, Ian D., "Isaiah 1–12: Presentation of a (Davidic?) Politics", in: A. Gow, P. Sabo (eds), *Tzedek, Tzedek Tirdof: Poetry, Prophecy, and Justice in Hebrew Scripture, FS Francis Landy* (BIS 137), Leiden 2017, 50–71.

Wöhrle, Jacob, *Die frühen Sammlungen des Zwölfprophetenbuches: Entstehung und Komposition* (BZAW 360), Berlin, New York 2006.

Wöhrle, Jacob, *Der Abschluss des Zwölfprophetenbuches: buchübergreifende Redaktionsprozesse in den späten Sammlungen* (BZAW 389), Berlin, New York 2008.

Wolff, Hans Walter, "Micah the Moreshite: The Prophet and his Background", in: J. G. Gammie (ed.), *Israelite Wisdom: Theological and Literary Essays in Honor of Samuel Terrien*, Missoula 1978, 77–84.

Wolff, Hans Walter, *Dodekapropheton 4 Micha* (BKAT XIV/4), Neukirchen-Vluyn 1982.

Wood, Joyce R., "Speech and Action in Micah's Prophecy", *CBQ* 62 (2000), 645–62

Woude, Adam S. van der, "Micah in Dispute with the Pseudo-Prophets", *VT* 19 (1969), 244–60.

Woude, Adam S. van der, "Micha 1:10–16", in: A. Caquot, M. Philonenko (eds), *Hommages à André Dupont-Sommer*, Paris 1971, 347–53.

Woude, Adam S. van der, „Deutero Micha: Ein Prophet aus Nord Israel", *NTT* 25 (1971), 365–378.

Woude, Adam S. van der, 'Micah IV 1–5: An Instance of the Pseudoprophets Quoting Isaiah', in: M. A. Beek et al (eds), *Symbolae Biblicae et Mesopotamicae, F. M. Th. de Liagre Böhl Dedicatae* (Studia Francisci Scholten Memoriae Dedicata 4), Leiden 1973, 396–402.

Woude, Adam S. van der, *Micha* (POT), Nijkerk 1976.

Woude, Adam S. van der, *Profeet en establishment: Een verklaring van het boek Micha*, Kampen 1985.

Younan, Mounib A., "Do Justice, Love Kindness, Walk Humbly: Just Peace in the Middle East", *The Ecumenical Review* 63 (2011), 25–34.

Zapff, Burkhard M., "The Book of Micah – the Theological Center of the Book of the Twelve", in: R. Albertz, J. D. Nogalski, J. Wöhrle (eds), *Perspectives on the Formation of the Book of the Twelve: Methodological Foundations-Redactional Processes-Historical Insights* (BZAW 433), Berlin, New York 2012), 129–40.

Zehnder, Markus, *Wegmetaphorik im Alten Testament: Eine semantische Untersuchung der alttestamentlichen und altorientalischen Weg-Lexeme mit besonderer Berücksichtigung ihrer metaphorischen Verwendung* (BZAW 268), Berlin 1999.

Zevit, Ziony, "The Common Origin of the Aramaicized Prayer to Horus and of Psalm 20", *JAOS* 110 (1990), 213–28.

Zgoll, Anette, "Innana and En-ḫedu-ana: Mutual Empowerment and the Myth Inanna Conquers Ur", in: K. Droß-Krüpe and S. Fink (eds), *Powerful Women in the Ancient World: Perception and (Self)Presentation, Proceedings of the 8th Melammu Workshop Kassel, 30 January – 1 February 2019* (Melammu Workshops and Monographs, 4), Münster 2021, 13–55.

Zimmerli, Walter, *Man and his Hope* (SBT,20), London ²1971.

Zimmermann, Kerstin, *Der Augsburger Religionsfrieden von 1555: Eine politische Lösung der Religions-problematik*, München 2010.

Index of Modern Authors

Ackerman, S. 103
Aimé-Giron, N. 115
Albertz, R. 37, 47, 59, 61, 91, 93
Andersen, F.I. 11, 22, 31, 42, 49–51, 53, 61, 95–96, 99–100, 107, 109, 118
Arneth, M. 40, 54
Asad, T. 51

Bail, U. 35, 49, 53
Banister, J. A. 121
Barstad, H.M. 47–49, 51–52, 57, 59, 61, 95
Bauman, Z 91
Becking, B. 10, 15, 28, 33, 38, 48, 50, 54, 57, 59, 65, 67, 97, 101, 116–17, 131
Benjamin, D.C. 57
Ben Zvi, E. 56, 67, 91, 95–96, 109
Blenkinsopp, J. 61, 93, 103
Block D.I. 50
Boloje, B.O. 115
Bonhoeffer, D. 101
Boogaart, T.A. 20, 35, 53, 67
Borger, R. 40
Bowen, N.R. 59
Bowie, F. 51
Bowman, R. 115
Brenner, A. 103
Brettler, M.Z 47
Brueggemann, W. 36, 47–48, 50–51, 121
Bruin, W.M. de, 107
Burkitt, F.C. 21, 81, 91, 105
Burnett, J.S. 61, 95

Carroll, M.D. 51
Carroll, R.P. 57, 61, 95
Cathcart, K.J. 23
Chapman, C.R. 110
Claassens, L.J.M. 103
Clifford, H. 47
Clines, D.J.A. 99–100
Colonna, M.-L. 110, 113
Collins, J. 11
Collins, T. 22, 35, 47, 53
Cooley, J.L. 59
Coppens, J. 16
Corzillius, B. 91

Cowley, A.E. 100
Craven, T. 103
Crum, W.E. 115
Cruz, J. 81, 87, 121
Cryer, F.C. 57, 118
Cuffey, K.H. 67–68, 91

Day, J. 123
Decorzant, A. 47, 61, 95
Deden, D. 16
Deller, K.H. 43
Dempsey, C.J. 22, 35, 42, 53
Dempster, S.G. 105
Deurloo, K.A. 15
Dever, W.G. 59
Dietrich, M. 32
Dietrich, W. 24, 101
Di Fransisco, L. 121
Dijk-Hemmes, F. van, 103
Dreisbach, D.L. 51, 61, 95

Ebeling, E. 32, 123
Edelkoort, A.H. 16–17
Eissfeldt, O. 21, 91
Enmarch, E. 41, 55
Esztári, R. 110–12

Falkenstein, A. 32
Feil, E. 100
Ferry, J. 67
Fischer, I. 103
Fohrer, G., 18
Foster, B.R. 123
Freedman, D.N. 11, 22, 31, 42, 49, 50–51, 53, 61, 95–96, 99–100, 107, 109, 118
Fritz, V. 52
Frymer-Kensky, T.S. 110, 113
Fuchs, E. 103

Gafney, W.C. 103
Garcia Martinez, F. 15
Geertz, C. 51
Gesenius, W. 100
Gilmour, G. 59
Goodman, N. 42

https://doi.org/10.1515/9783111208657-016

Gordis, R. 133
Gordon, R.P. 131–33
Grayson, A.K. 39
Grey, J. 103
Grollenberg, L. 15
Groot, A. de, 16
Gruber, M.I 105, 110
Gunkel, H. 27

Hagedorn, A.C. 10, 25
Hagstrom, D.G. 22, 35, 53, 57, 67
Halton, C. 59
Hamori, E.J. 103
Handy, L.K. 129
Hargrove, B. 51
Harris, R. 110, 113
Harvey, J. 92
Heckl, R. 116, 125
Heiser, M. 48
Helle, S. 111
Hillers, D.R. 31, 35–36, 42–43, 45, 47, 49–53,
    56–59, 61, 67–68, 73, 95–96, 100, 107, 119
Holm, T.L. 115
Holter, K. 59
Horst, P.W. van der, 131
Hout, C.F.M. van den, 25
Hubbard, R.L. 51
Hume, D. 90
Hutton, J.M. 48
Hyatt, J.Ph. 100
Hyman, R.T. 95, 101

Jacobs, M.R. 31, 35–36, 50–51, 53, 67–68, 95–
    96, 100
Janzen, W. 45, 119
Jeffers, A. 57, 118
Jensen, J. 100
Jensen, R.R. 49, 92
Jenson, P.P. 121
Jeppesen, K. 32, 51, 58
Jeremias, J. 21–22, 31, 35, 47, 49, 53, 56–57, 61,
    67, 95–96, 121
Ji, H.-W. 51
Jones, B.A. 47
Jong, M. de, 42-43, 46, 57, 110, 118
Jong Ellis, M. de, 39, 54
Joosten, J. 92, 100

Kakabadse, N.K. 51, 101
Kämmerer, Th.R. 123
Kautzsch, E. 100
Kessler, R. 22, 31, 35, 42, 49–53, 55–58, 61, 64,
    67, 92, 95–96, 100–01, 121
Kister, M. 125
Klein, L.R. 103
Knierim, R. 50
Konstantopoulos, G. 118
Korpel, M.C.A. 26, 33, 118
Korte, A.-M. 103
Kosmala, H. 36, 50, 68
Kottsieper, I. 125, 128
Kraemer, R.S. 103
Krašovec, J. 127
Kratz, R.G 23, 56
Kuhrt, A. 41, 55

Labahn, A. 67
Labuschagne, C.J. 21–22, 25, 47–48, 121–22, 124
Lambert, W.G. 39
Landy, F. 91
Lang, B. 48, 92
LeCureux, J.T. 10, 25, 67
Leene, H. 63, 67
Lemche, N.P. 61, 93
Lescow, Th. 21
Leuenberger, M. 129
Levin, C. 63–69
Lewis, T.J. 113, 121–22, 124
Liagre Böhl, F.M.Th. de, 131–33
Lichtheim, M. 124
Longman, T. 11, 39, 54
Lundbom, J.R. 65
Lyotard, J.F. 91

Mastnjak, N. 65–66
Maul, S.M. 59
May, N.N. 110–12
Mays, J.L. 22, 35, 53, 67, 91, 96, 100
McKane, W. 22, 35, 49, 53, 64, 67, 96, 100
Mendez, H.E. 59
Merk, O. 23
Mettinger, T.N.D. 59
Metzler, K.A. 12
Meyers, C.L. 103
Meyer, E.E. 99
Middlemas, J. 121–22, 124

Miller, P.D. 56
Monroe, L.A.S. 61, 93
Moor, J.C. de, 25–27, 56, 61, 94–96, 104, 107, 109, 118, 121, 132
Mostovicz, E.I. 51, 101
Mowinckel, S. 38

Na'aman, N. 61
Nasuti, H.P. 56
Nelson, R.D. 38, 54
Neujahr, M. 54
Newberry, P.E. 115
Newman, L.E. 39
Nicholson, E.W. 59
Nielsen, K. 82, 92
Nims, C.F. 115–17, 125–28
Nissinen, M. 28, 33, 43, 57, 103, 110, 112, 117
Noegel, S.B. 118
Nogalski, J.L. 10, 23–24, 35, 47, 53, 67, 92, 105, 107
Noort, E. 15

O'Brien, J.M. 9, 91, 95, 97, 100
O'Connor, M.P. 99–100
Oesch, J. 25
Olmo Lete, G. del, 132
Olson, D.T. 47
Olyan, S.M. 48, 59, 119
Otto, E. 56

Paas, S. 25
Pardee, D. 59, 125
Pardes, I. 103
Park, S.J. 60
Parpola, S., 33, 42, 110, 112–13
Peacock, K.C. 47, 61
Peels, H.G.L. 125
Penchansky, D. 48
Perroudon, M.-C. 112
Petersen, D.L. 103
Pfälzner, P. 59
Philip, L.B. 15
Pongratz-Leisten, B. 115
Prinsloo, G.T.M. 125
Pryke, L.M. 110

Redditt, P.L. 47
Reiner, E. 59

Richelle, M. 53
Ridderbos, J. 16
Römer, Th.C. 38, 54
Rösel, M. 125, 127
Rogan, J. 9
Roth, M. 47, 60, 92
Rudman, D. 36, 49, 64
Runions, E. 35, 53, 87, 100, 109, 118

Sanders, P. 121, 130
Sandman, M. 124
Saracino, F. 131–33
Savran, G.W. 32
Scaiola, D 121
Schart, A. 10, 24, 47, 67
Schmid, K. 38
Schmidt, B.B. 59
Schmidt, L. 60, 95
Schmitt, R. 59
Schoors, A. 99
Scriba, A. 32
Schütte, W. 105
Schultz, R.L. 67
Schuman, N.A. 15
Sedlmeier, F. 65
Selms, A. van, 18
Sjöberg, Å.W. 111
Smith, J.Z. 51
Smith, M. 50
Smith, M.S. 59
Smith, R.L. 107, 121
Smith-Christopher, D.L. 35–36, 50, 53
Sommer, B. 67
Spek, R.J. van der, 55
Stansell, G. 56, 58
Stavrakopoulou, F. 59, 113
Steiner, R.C. 115–17, 125–28
Steinert, U. 111
Steymans, H.U. 28, 44
Stökl, J. 57, 103, 110–12
Streck, M. 28, 44
Strydom, J.G. 20, 35, 53, 67, 92
Sweeney, M.A. 35–36, 49, 64, 97, 100

Talon, Ph. 12
Talstra, E. 65
Tietz, C. 100
Toorn, K. van der, 11, 42, 57, 115–18, 125–29, 131

Torrance, T.F. 31, 51, 61, 95
Tsukimoto, A. 59

Utzschneider, H. 22, 35–36, 50, 53, 68

Valdez, S. 9
Vér, Á. 110–12
Vleeming, S.P. 115, 125, 127
Vos, D. de, 15
Vries, S.J. de, 15
Vriezen, Th.C. 15–16, 21, 31, 35

Wagenaar, J.A. 21–22, 25, 34–36, 49–50, 53, 56–57, 67–68, 105, 119, 131–33
Wagner, V. 56
Wal, A.J.O. van der, 23–24
Walsh, L. 57
Waltke, B.K. 31, 35, 42–43, 51, 53, 95–96, 99–100, 107, 121
Weber, M 101
Weippert, M 110, 112
Wellhausen, J. 9–11, 20, 22, 35, 53, 67, 73
Wells, B. 56
Werner, W. 51, 61, 95

Wesselius, J.W. 115, 125, 127
Wessels, W. 53
Westenholz, J.G. 111
Westermann, C. 119
Williamson, H.G.M. 69
Willi-Plein, I. 21
Willis, J.T. 21, 58, 68, 91, 97, 106–07
Wilson, I.D. 75
Wöhrle, J. 10, 25, 31, 47, 51, 67, 92, 121
Woerden, M. van, 15
Wolff, H.W. 16, 47, 91–92, 96, 100–01
Wood, J.R. 22, 35, 42, 45, 53, 57
Woude, A.S. van der, 9, 12, 15, 17–21, 22, 25, 28, 31, 35–37, 42–43, 47, 49, 53, 56–58, 60–61, 64, 67, 73, 91–92, 95–96, 100, 105, 107, 118

Younan, M.A. 51

Zapff, B.M. 10, 25, 67
Zehnder, M. 26
Zevit, Z. 125
Zgoll, A. 111
Zimmerli, W. 36, 50
Zimmermann, K. 50

Index of Sources

Hebrew Bible

Genesis
1:7 82
22:17 128

Exodus
15:11 122
17:7 82
34:6 87, 121

Leviticus
25 56

Numeri
12:6 118
22–24 60, 95

Deuteronomy
4:16,23,25 59
7:5 60
12:3 60
13:1–5 118
15:1 ff 56
16:1 60
18:10 59
21:5 82
27:15 59
28 78
29 68
29:23–25 66
30:15–16 98–99

Joshua
3:1 61, 95
4:19 61, 95

Judges
6:25–30 60
12:2 82

2 Samuel
1:20 107
15:2 82

1 Kings
8 66
9 68
9:8–9 67
18:18 60

2 Kings
17 10
17:16 60
21:7 59
22–23 61, 93

Isaiah
1–39 46
1 69
1:2 33
1:28–31 69
2–12 69
2 15–16, 20, 49, 64
2:2–5 69
5:5 108
8:9 33
10 79
40–66 9
51:22 109
60:19 109

Jeremiah
2:32 39
8:4 39
15:1 82
18:14 39
21:1–23:40 65
22 68
22:6–7 65
22:8–9 65–66
22:8 65–66
23:8 118
25:31 82–83
26 20, 22, 35, 53, 73
30–31 11, 38, 63
31:27.31.38 38
50:35 83

https://doi.org/10.1515/9783111208657-017

Ezekiel
44:24 82

Hosea
4:1 83

Amos
1:11 129
3:1 33
6:12 39

Obadiah
12 107

Micah
1–5 21, 81, 87, 89
1 18–19, 23, 28, 31, 51–52, 71–72, 82
1:2–7 18
1:2 32, 72, 85
1:3–4 32
1:3 85
1:5 52
1:6 72, 85
1:7 52, 85
1:8–16 18
1:8 72, 87, 104
1:10–16 72
1:15 72, 85
2–3 23
2–5 9–11, 17, 19–20, 22–23, 25, 28, 31, 34–43,
      50–52, 60, 65, 67–68, 71, 73–77, 91, 104–05
2:1–13 26–27
2:1–5 73, 119
2:1–2 56
2:3 73, 85
2:6–11 17
2:7 87
2:8–9 73
2:10 73
2:12–13 83
2:12 23, 73, 82–85
2:13 73, 85
3 57, 69, 74, 87
3:1 32, 57
3:4 86, 88
3:5–8 74, 118
3:5–6 57
3:5 86

3:6 42
3:7 86, 88
3:8* 23, 58
3:9–4:5 67–69
3:9–12 68, 74
3:9 57
3:12 15, 19, 34, 52, 65, 76
4 10, 16, 20, 63–69
4:1–5 23, 68
4:1–4 19, 34, 49–53, 63–69, 74–76
4:2–5 15
4:2 66, 86
4:3 86
4:5 48–49, 98
4:6–7 75
4:6–7a.8 23
4:6 86
4:7 86
4:8–14 76
4:13 75
4:9–10.14 23
4:10 86
4:11–14 22
4:12 86
5 17, 31, 51, 58–59
5:1 31, 51
5:1–6 75
5:1–4a 23
5:2 75
5:4 23, 131–33
5:4b-5 131–33
5:6–8 84
5:7 75, 82, 84
5:9–14 75, 76
5:9–13 23, 58
5:9 86
5:10 86
5:11 86
5:12 86
5:13 76, 86
5:14 58, 86, 88–90
6–7 20–21, 23, 28, 31, 43–45, 51, 60, 71, 77–79,
      81–90, 91–101, 104–06, 110
6 82, 94–96
6:1–16 81
6:1–8 60, 78–79, 92–94, 96
6:1–2 96–97
6:1 32, 88

6:2 88
6:3–8 97
6:3–5 95
6:3 89
6:4 88
6:5–6 60
6:7–8 95
6:7 89
6:8 15, 29, 31, 51, 61, 78, 88, 91–101
6:9–16 78–79, 94, 96–97
6:9 117–18
6:13 88
6:14–15 28, 44–45, 78, 97
6:16 88, 98
7 61
7:1–7 45
7:1–6 27, 78–79, 109
7:4 45
7:6 45
7:7–20 105–06
7:7–14 81
7:7–10 16
7:7 89
7:8–20 45
7:8–13 103–13
7:8–10 105
7:8–9 87
7:9 88–89
7:11–13 79, 105
7:10 27, 109
7:14–17 84, 105
7:14 81–82, 84
7:16–17 79
7:17 46
7:18–20 47, 120–21
7:18 47, 89, 121
7:19–20 121
7:19 89
7:20 89

Nahum
1:12 129

Proverbs
11:2 100

Psalms
19:1–5 128
20 115, 125
35:19, 24 107
38:17 107
68:8–10 122
81:4 125
88:5 128
104 123
137 107
146:3 10

Job
21:4 87
24:21 133

Ecclesiastes
3 9

Ruth
1:6 109

Song of Songs
1:8 129

Ezra
1 41

Sirach
16:25 100
35:3 100

Mesopotamian Texts

Assurbanipal
Annals
  IX:65–67 44
Hymn to Ishtar of Nineveh
  SAA 3.7:4–8 111

Autobiography of Marduk
40

BIN
  I 36:23 107

City Lament Urim
265–274 45

Coronation hymn of Ashurbanipal
SAA III 11
Rev. 9–10 40, 54–55

Cyrus Cylinder
11–14 41
30–34 41

Enuma Elish
IV:3–8 12

Erra Epic
IV 56–58 109

Esarhaddon
Loyalty Oaths *VTE* = SAA II
6:429–30 28, 44

Hymn to Marduk
K. 3351
16 32

KAR
19
1–16 123
298
Rev. 17 132
421
ii:11'-14' 39
iii:1'-8' 39
rev. ii:18'-20' 39

LB
2001 131–32

Neo-Assyrian Prophecies
SAA IX
1 iv:40' 112
1 v 112
2 ii:35' 112
2 ii:30–37 33
3 i:27-ii:2 33

Neo-Babylonian *kudurru*
V. R. 56 = *BBS*, VI
ii 51–60 28, 44

Sennacherib
Annals Rassam Cylinder
IX:65–67 28

Sumerian Hymns
CBS 13936 (STVC 35)
58–63 32

**Treaty of Aššur-nerari with Mati'-ilu,
the king of Arpad**
SAA III 2
ii: rev. 8–14 120
iv:8–12 46

UET
4 184:15 107

UM
29–16–229 ii 4f 109

Urad-Gula Letter
SAA X 294
Rev. 30–33 43, 57

Ugaritic Texts

KTU
1.3
v:32 124
1.4
iv:41–43 124
v:3–4 124

vii:43–44 127
viii:1–32 32
1.10
i:3–5 128
1.107
44–45 132

Egyptian Texts

Aten Hymn
78–82 123–24

Ipuwer
8,1–5 41, 55

Sinuhe
81–84 37

Aramaic Texts

Elephantine
TAD D5:6 127

Papyrus Amherst 63
115–30
i–v 116
vi–xi 116
vii:12–17 117
xi:8–13 117–18
xii–xiii 116
xii:10 127
xii:11–19 115, 125

xiii:1–10 125
xiii:6 125
xiii:11–17 125–28
xiv–xvii 116
xviii–xxiii 116
xx:9 127
xii:1.6.7.15 127

Zakkur of Hamath
KAI 202
A:10 127
A:13 117

Qumran

4Q216
2:19 128

New Testament

Matthew 2:6 31, 51

Index of Subjects

Aaron 60
Adonay 127
Ahab, king 97
Anat 59
Anger 89
Asherah 48, 59
Ashurbanipal 54–55, 116
Assyria 107
Aten 123–24

Baal 124, 126, 129, 131
Babylonian Exile 16, 35
Balaam 60
Bashan 105
Bayâ 111–12
Bes 131
Biters 131–33
Bonhoeffer, Dietrich 101
Breaker(s) 74, 132–33

Carmel 105
Compassion 89
Confidence 105
cuius regio, eius religio 50
Cyrus Cylinder 41, 55

Deborah 103
Delight 89
Demon(s) 131–33
Divine Spitit 16
Doxology 47–48
Dream report 117–18

Edom 107
Elijah 131
Eros 131
Ethics 91–101
Evil spirits 133
Exile 64
Exodus 60, 95

Fear not! 117–18
Female Prophet 109
Fidelity 89

Flock 81–84
Frenzy 110–12
Futility clauses 43–44, 78–79, 97

Gebot der Stunde 101
Gender 103–13
Gilead 105
Gloating 107
Good times and Bad times 11, 75

Heilszeitherrscher 75
Hulda 103
Humble 100

Iaa, land 37, 66
Ilu 124
Illusa-Amur 111–12
Impatient 87
Incantation 131–3
Incomparability 47–48, 89, 120–29
Individualization 91
Ishtar 59, 110–12

Jan van Eyck 15
Jerusalem 109
Josiah, king 60, 91–93

Lachish 18
Lawsuit 95
Long suffering 87
Loving kindness 89

Maccabean Age 105
Mar/Mara 116–17
Marduk 123
Maria 131
Messiah 17, 31, 51
Metaphor 81–90
Miriam 60, 103
Monolatrism 124
Moon 131
Morality 50–51, 60–61
Moses 60, 131
Mulissu 110

https://doi.org/10.1515/9783111208657-018

Netherworld 131
New age 35
New moon 125
Noomi 109
Numerology 21–22

Omri, king 97
Osiris 131

Papyrus Amherst 63 115–30
Pericope 26–27
Personal Computer 23–24
Phoenix 128
Prophecies/ Oracles of doom 9, 15, 18–19, 34–43, 52–54, 65, 72–76, 105
Prophecies/ Oracles of Salvation 9, 34–43, 52–54, 65, 73–76, 105
Prophetic formula 116-
Prophetic futurology 34–43, 51, 53–55, 73–76
Pseudo-prophets 19–20, 57–58
Puns 71

Ra 131
Redaktionsgeschichte 10–11, 24–26
Remnant 81–2

Shamash 54, 123
Shamas-shumu-ukin 116
Shepherd 84
Sibitti 133
Sorcery 59

Theatre 63–69
Theophany 31–32, 52, 72

Urad Gula 42

Woe-oracle 45, 73, 119
World War II 15, 91

Zeus 131